JB JOSSEY-BASS™
A Wiley Brand

T0314185

Volunteer Training Primer

Principles, Procedures and Ideas for Training and Educating Volunteers

Scott C. Stevenson, Editor

WILEY

Copyright © 2009 by John Wiley & Sons, Inc. All rights reserved.

Originally published by Stevenson, Inc.

Published by John Wiley & Sons, Inc., Hoboken, New Jersey.

No part of this publication may be reproduced, stored in a retrieval system, or transmitted in any form or by any means, electronic, mechanical, photocopying, recording, scanning, or otherwise, except as permitted under Section 107 or 108 of the 1976 United States Copyright Act, without either the prior written permission of the Publisher, or authorization through payment of the appropriate per-copy fee to the Copyright Clearance Center, Inc., 222 Rosewood Drive, Danvers, MA 01923, (978) 750-8400, fax (978) 646-8600, or on the Web at www.copyright.com. Requests to the Publisher for permission should be addressed to the Permissions Department, John Wiley & Sons, Inc., 111 River Street, Hoboken, NJ 07030, (201) 748-6011, fax (201) 748-6008, or online at http://www.wiley.com/go/permissions.

Limit of Liability/Disclaimer of Warranty: While the publisher and author have used their best efforts in preparing this book, they make no representations or warranties with respect to the accuracy or completeness of the contents of this book and specifically disclaim any implied warranties of merchantability or fitness for a particular purpose. No warranty may be created or extended by sales representatives or written sales materials. The advice and strategies contained herein may not be suitable for your situation. You should consult with a professional where appropriate. Neither the publisher nor author shall be liable for any loss of profit or any other commercial damages, including but not limited to special, incidental, consequential, or other damages.

For general information on our other products and services or for technical support, please contact our Customer Care Department within the United States at (800) 762-2974, outside the United States at (317) 572-3993 or fax (317) 572-4002.

Wiley publishes in a variety of print and electronic formats and by print-on-demand. Some material included with standard print versions of this book may not be included in e-books or in print-on-demand. If this book refers to media such as a CD or DVD that is not included in the version you purchased, you may download this material at http://booksupport.wiley.com. For more information about Wiley products, visit www.wiley.com.

978-1-118-69209-7   ISBN

978-1-118-70419-6   ISBN (online)

Volunteer Training Primer

Principles, Procedures and Ideas
for Training and Educating Volunteers

Published by

Stevenson, Inc.

P.O. Box 4528 • Sioux City, Iowa • 51104
Phone 712.239.3010 • Fax 712.239.2166
www.stevensoninc.com

© 2009 by Stevenson, Inc. All rights reserved by the publisher. No part of this publication may be reproduced or transmitted in any form or by any means, electronic or mechanical, including photocopying, recording, or any other information storage or retrieval system, without written permission of the publisher. Violators will be prosecuted. This publication is designed to provide accurate and authoritative information in regard to the subject matter covered. It is sold with the understanding that the publisher is not engaged in legal, accounting or other professional services. If legal or other expert assistance is required, the services of a competent professional person should be sought. (From a Declaration of Principles jointly adopted by a committee of the American Bar Association and a committee of publishers.) Stevenson, Inc., does not necessarily endorse any products or services mentioned.

TABLE OF CONTENTS

Volunteer Training Primer

TABLE OF CONTENTS

ORIENTATION & TRAINING BASICS

Do new volunteers coming on board really know much about your organization and its history? Training is one thing, but education that goes beyond the job is equally important. Make orientation a standard procedure for all new volunteers. It's also important to convey key expectations up front and to cover particular topics that may be universal for all your volunteers: confidentiality issues, showing up on time, time management and more.

Electronic Orientation Overcomes Scheduling Woes

One of the main challenges The Chester County Hospital's volunteer services office (West Chester, PA) faces when welcoming a new volunteer is scheduling orientation. Two obstacles hamper timely orientation attendance: scheduling a convenient time for day, evening and weekend volunteers, and the consumption of the staff and volunteers' time.

Using the power of a computer, the volunteer services staff found a solution to their problem — an electronic version of a volunteer orientation. Staff burned a CD of a PowerPoint presentation covering the hospital's mandatory topics (e.g., fire safety, HIPPA, infection control, patient safety and volunteer policies such as dress code and attendance). Short video clips were also embedded in the presentation to demonstrate hand-washing techniques and wheelchair safety. After each section, volunteers complete a short self-test on information they viewed in the orientation presentation. The completed test is filed in each volunteer's personnel file as confirmation of attendance. Volunteers receive a hard copy of the presentation, a customer service tip sheet, fire and disaster procedures, and personal security tips as take-home support material.

The CD presentation allows increased flexibility for volunteers and staff. Volunteers view the presentation at their own pace, allowing for better comprehension of the material. Most volunteers complete the orientation in around 45 minutes. Volunteers may either view the orientation at volunteer services where a staff person is available to answer questions and assist volunteers who are not computer savvy, or the CD may be taken home.

"The electronic orientation presentation provides the opportunity to complete an obligation that would otherwise be daunting and time consuming in a more timely and convenient pace for hospital volunteers," says Kathy Stocker, director of volunteer services.

Source: Kathy Stocker, Director of Volunteer Services, The Chester County Hospital, West Chester, PA. Phone (610) 431-5191. E-mail: kstocker@cchosp.com

Integrate Your Agency's History Into Volunteer Training

Fueling passions about your organization, giving volunteers a sense of pride and ownership, creating connections and helping volunteers do their job better are all great reasons why you should consider sharing your organization's history with your volunteers.

For example:

- During orientation, every volunteer at the Idaho Elks Rehabilitation Hospital (Boise, ID) watches a 15-minute video, put together in house by the development director, that shows the beginnings of the hospital started in the founder's home to its current state. Sandi Borup, volunteer coordinator, says the video, combined with a brief overview from the hospital administrator, helps fuel the volunteers' passion for working at the hospital. "It shows what we're all about," she says. "We're a unique facility and knowing our history helps instill a sense of pride in our volunteers."

- Volunteers for the Huntington Library, Art Collections and Botanical Gardens (San Marino, CA) receive a 200-page book, written by a former director, about the organization's history. Mikki Heydorff, education, volunteer programs manager, says knowing this history helps the volunteers do the best job possible when showing the grounds and collections to visitors and students. "They need to know who the founders are and why they chose the collections they did. The volunteer's role is preserving those collections and sharing them with the public," she says. Heydorff also says sharing the history with volunteers creates a vested interest in the organization. The volunteers feel like they're part of the family and tend to stay longer.

Source: Sandi Borup, Volunteer Coordinator, Idaho Elks Rehabilitation Hospital, Boise, ID. Phone (208) 489-4916. E-mail: sborup@ierh.org
Mikki Heydorff, Education, Volunteer Programs Manager, Huntington Library, Art Collections and Botanical Gardens, San Marino, CA. Phone (626) 405-2126. E-mail: mheydorff@huntington.org

How to Teach a Skill

- When teaching others how to perform a skill, be able to perform that skill well. Work out a series of steps that helps participants master the skill. Encourage striving for accuracy rather than speed.

ORIENTATION & TRAINING BASICS

Do Your Volunteers Really Know Your Organization?

Sometimes in the rush to get help, organizations will put volunteers to work without giving them all the information they really need. Volunteers are not only workers but also ambassadors and, as such, need to be well informed.

Share the following information to help your volunteers be effective ambassadors:

Share your organization's history — Having an historical timeline of the organization will help new volunteers know how it has evolved.

Mission statement — Insure that each new volunteer, no matter what his or her position, knows the mission statement. Knowing the purpose of the organization is essential to performing any job and in explaining the organization to others.

Organizational chart — Give each new volunteer an organizational chart. It's important that everyone in the group, including volunteers, knows who is in charge of each area and where they fit in the mix. Volunteers need to know to whom they should go when they have questions or when they need help. Not knowing who's in charge will lead to frustration that in turn can lead to losing volunteer help.

Get People to Show Up for Orientation

Need some help getting people to show up for orientation? Perhaps one or more of these techniques will increase the percentage of participants:

1. **Make orientation a condition of volunteering.** Have new volunteers sign off on a statement saying they will participate in orientation at the time they agree to volunteer.

2. **Reward those who do participate.** Offer some incentive that makes it more attractive to show up: free tickets, a discount coupon, bonus hours that count toward prizes, etc.

3. **Stress the importance of participation.** Make it obvious that job fulfillment can't occur without participating in orientation procedures.

Time Management Training: 'Give Me One More Minute!'

Everyone struggles with using time effectively. When you can't get a grip on time management, productivity decreases and self-doubt about performance can increase.

Kit Prendergast, certified career management coach, Career Connections of Sierra Nevada (Reno, NV), says a direct link exists between time management and the psychological, emotional and physical energy you put into your work. In other words, we do our best work when our energy is high. So if we plan our day around that energy, we will get more done.

To make the most out of a workday, Prendergast suggests, first determine what a really good work day looks like to you. Ask yourself: "When am I at my best?" Hook into when you are at your best and what helps to contribute to that positive work situation. Try to replicate it.

Also, determine the value you bring to your organization when you use your time and energy well, and strive to maximize that value.

Here are some tips to get back that time and energy:

1. **Establish a rhythm to your day.** Be conscious of the periods of high energy and design the flow of your day to maximize those windows of opportunity, with short breaks. For example, take the first 45 minutes of an hour for tasks that require concentration and use the last 15 minutes for quick jobs, like checking e-mail.

2. **Prioritize your work.** Set up a plan for what needs to be done first. Ask yourself, "What could I achieve this morning that would really put me in great shape for the rest of the day?"

3. **Create more time.** Quit multi-tasking and break the e-mail addiction. When you multi-task, you actually lose concentration and can end up wasting your energy-efficient windows of opportunity. Those little bits of time that take away from your work (constantly checking your e-mail) can really add up. Set a designated time for these little tasks, like checking e-mail at only certain times within the hour.

4. **Reduce three big time wasters:** perfectionism, procrastination and interruptions. Rethink your tendency to make your work perfect, which can lead to procrastinating on a project. Develop a plan to tactfully reduce interruptions and share it with colleagues and volunteers. For example, set up office hours during which volunteers can just walk in and where your full time and attention can be given to them.

5. **Make more space.** Clutter in your physical environment can drain your energy. By de-cluttering, you can create a better psychological space for yourself.

Source: Katherine (Kit) Prendergast, CCMC, Certified Career Management Coach, Career Connections of Sierra Nevada, Reno, NV. Phone (775) 324-5151.
E-mail: kit@careerconnectionsSN.com

ORIENTATION & TRAINING BASICS

Spell Out Attendance Expectations

If attendance at meetings is an issue for your organization, perhaps you should add more detail to your policy. Some examples might include:

- Absences versus excused absences.
- Number of meetings one can miss throughout the year.
- Number of missed meetings in a row.

- Consequences for absenteeism.
- Rewards/recognition for perfect attendance.

Find out how other organizations in your community address attendance at meetings as you add more detail to your own expectations.

16 Rules and Regulations Worth Sharing With Volunteers

Giving your volunteers written rules and regulations to your organization helps clear away any questions they may have and clarifies what is expected of them. In doing so, Rita Chick, director, American Red Cross/Bay Area Chapter in San Francisco, suggests you include this information, and explains why:

1. **Welcome letter from CEO, chairman of the board** — A welcoming note helps get volunteers geared up and acknowledge them for their services.

2. **Mission of your organization** — Explains the big picture, a mantra of the goals your organization is striving to reach.

3. **General organization information:**
   a. Maps — Not only of the headquarters but where the volunteer will be doing service, if in a different location.
   b. Organizational chart — Who to go to for help, the next on the chain of command and who to solicit for advice.
   c. Building evacuation plan — Safety issues are always important and vary from geographical location. Be sure you cover all possible emergency scenarios for the safe removal of your volunteers and staff.

4. **Benefits to volunteering at your organization** — Reminds the volunteers what they do for the organization and what they do for themselves, intrinsically.

5. **What your organization expects from volunteers** — Provides a platform of ideals and expectations, such as being respectful, treating information with confidentiality, maintaining a professional manner and dressing appropriately for the task.

6. **What volunteers can expect from the organization** — For many it is a source of socialization, education and career development. Volunteers can expect to be treated with respect by all staff members and participants of the organization.

7. **Insurance information** — Varies per organization, but the pamphlet should discuss liability issues such as accidents while on site, driving and other issues.

8. **Tax deduction information** — Provides information that volunteers can further discuss with their tax accountants. For example, mileage to and from the organization may be deductible.

9. **Criteria for driving** — Informs volunteers of the licensing laws, including licenses for operating specific vehicles. If you require a check on a volunteer's driving record, you will need him/her to sign a form allowing your state's department of motor vehicles to provide that information to you.

10. **Criteria for a negative criminal background check** — If the background check comes back with information that can set your organization, staff and/or participants at risk, inform the volunteer candidates they cannot serve in those capacities.

11. **Code of conduct** — Reiterates that volunteers must conduct themselves in a courteous, respectful and professional manner.

12. **Policy on violence and sexual harassment in the workplace** — Informs the volunteer candidates of the consequences of these issues and the actions they should take should such a situation ever arise.

13. **Dress code** — Informs the volunteer when and what dress is appropriate.

14. **Identification policy** — Who should wear name tags? This details when and why.

15. **Personnel record** — Explains why records are kept confidential and make it crystal clear to the volunteer who is handling confidential information and who is not privy to it.

16. **Training records** — Information for staff and volunteers to help with training and logistic moves from one organization to another.

ORIENTATION & TRAINING BASICS

Give New Volunteers A Helping Hand

- Provide directions to your facility or office. If your location is even somewhat obscure, provide new recruits with printed directions to your facility or meeting place.
- Host an employee reception for a group of new volunteers at the end of your work day. Give both staff and volunteers a chance to meet and get to know one another early on.
- Provide a complete tour of your facilities. Volunteers will have a better understanding of how their jobs fit into the big picture if they know what the big picture looks and feels like.

Pre-cross-training Steps

Before making the leap to cross-train all volunteers — so each can do others' jobs — give your volunteers a taste of what others are doing. Have them observe others in action to determine if that's something they would enjoy or with which they would be willing to assist.

To allow formal observation of other volunteers on the job, set up a once-a-month schedule that "spotlights" key positions. Publicize each monthly spotlight among your volunteers and invite those interested to assemble on the designated date to observe the volunteer(s) in action and ask questions they might have about the job duties.

Sharing a taste of volunteering opportunities helps volunteers make wiser decisions about jobs they select.

How to Prepare Volunteers to Safeguard Confidentiality

Do your volunteers work with confidential patient or student records, donor information, assessment forms, referral forms or computer records?

If so, you need to impress the importance of respecting confidentiality with new volunteers upon recruiting them. You may want to cover this issue during orientation. Make sure volunteers know that it's possible, even likely, that they'll feel pressure to discuss confidential information. Communicate your organization's policy on the matter. Consider having them sign a confidentiality agreement.

Managing the situation after it arises is much more difficult. Given human nature, it may be unrealistic to expect volunteers not to talk with one another and/or share information about your organization with others outside of your organization.

The most important thing is to focus on building a sense of community and inclusion that discourages volunteers from disclosing information that could harm your organization. Think about what you offer that compels volunteers to stay at your organization. What advantages/incentives do you offer that encourage volunteers to maintain confidentiality? Volunteers who are happy, challenged and respected are much less likely to engage in behavior that raises suspicion.

Reinforce Confidentiality Among Volunteer Ranks

Many volunteer positions require high levels of confidentiality. In those circumstances, what are you doing to get the message across to volunteers?

Volunteers will be more aware of the need to maintain confidentiality if you convey its importance often and in various ways. Some ideas for doing so:

- Include a confidentiality statement in volunteer position descriptions.

- Go over specific confidentiality instructions during orientation and include them in your handbook.

- Reiterate the need for confidentiality as volunteers begin new jobs.

- Post signs regarding the need for confidentiality, and make mention of it in written communications.

- Point out consequences for not adhering to confidentiality.

ORIENTATION & TRAINING BASICS

Look to State and National Organizations for Training

If you're new to the field of volunteer management, look to national and state organizations in your agency's field to cover on-the-job training.

For example, Sandra Owens, volunteer coordinator, St. John's Hospice Care (Springfield, MO), sits on the State Hospice Volunteer Coordinator's Committee. The committee, which is part of Missouri Hospice and Palliative Care, holds regional training conferences annually.

The sessions, taught by seasoned volunteer coordinators with help from the state organization, cover topics from recruiting, training, supervision, retention and risk management. "This also helps to keep the 'trainers' learning," says Owens.

National organizations, like National Hospice and Palliative Care Organization (www.nhpco), hold trainings around the country for volunteers and coordinators.

Source: Sandra Owens, Volunteer Coordinator, St. John's Hospice Care, Springfield, MO. Phone (417) 820-7550. E-mail: sjowens@sprg.mercy.net

Entertaining Board Orientation Grabs Attention, Interest

Orientation meetings for new board members don't need to be boring experiences.

While it's important for your new board members to become familiar with the goals, programs and history of your organization, learning about and discovering these things can be entertaining, informative and involve some friendly competition.

Try some of these ideas to make your next meeting of new board members an anticipated occasion:

Trivial Pursuit — Use a computer graphics program to make cards, game pieces and a board so any number of players can correctly answer the most questions (both important facts and fun bits of trivia) about your organization.

Six degrees of separation — Take a "family tree" approach to an activity where new board members create a chart, starting with how they first became familiar with your institution. Points can be earned by naming the most people who have been involved as supporters, or for tracing family involvement back the longest.

Audio and visual flash cards — Make tapes and/or slides of various departments and activities within your facility, then see which new board member will be first to answer which program or job is being shown. Follow the game with a brief tour of some of those areas and some introductions to department heads.

Trolley tour and box lunch — If your institution has buildings in a widespread radius in the same city, or if you have a large campus, treat your guests to a guided tour as if they are visiting a new place with historic landmarks. Provide an old-fashioned portable lunch, either on the trolley or bus or in a pleasant setting at one of the sites on the route.

Present a short play — Use talented volunteers or staff who like to perform to give a fun "recital" with the plot revolving around historical events, current activities and future goals. Recruit your best volunteer researchers to gather facts, your best writers to complete the script, and the best amateur musicians, singers and actors you can find.

Even if an ordinary all-business meeting and facility tour is still required, your new board members will look forward to some unexpected fun with the hard work.

Establish Quantifiable Objectives for Volunteers

Whether you're planning a single project that involves volunteers or developing a comprehensive operational plan for the upcoming year, it's in everyone's best interest to establish quantifiable objectives for volunteers. In fact, you will be further ahead if you can work with the volunteers involved to draft those objectives together. The more involved they are in their development, the more likely volunteers are to "own" them and follow through on them.

Here are examples of quantifiable objectives developed for either individual volunteers or group volunteers:

- Recruit five new volunteers during the course of the year.
- Attend a minimum of 10 out of 12 regularly scheduled meetings during the year.
- Volunteer for at least one project without being asked.
- Complete assigned campaign calls within the two-week time frame.
- Contribute a minimum of two hours each month throughout the fiscal year.
- Sell a minimum of 20 tickets per volunteer one week prior to the event.
- Identify at least three cost-saving ideas for the agency during the course of the year.
- Coordinate one new special event during the fiscal year.

Examine what it is you most want your volunteers to accomplish, then break it down into achievable (and quantifiable) parts. They will be more likely to succeed if expectations are clear.

ORIENTATION & TRAINING BASICS

Exercise in Project Management Will Help Get Yours Off the Ground

Have you ever tackled a project that turned out to be fraught with problems, or simply put off making a change because the task seemed too complicated?

Kathleen McCleskey of KM Consulting and Training Connection (Austin, TX) offers a project planning tool that will almost assure success.

"The more effort spent in planning, the easier the project," McCleskey says. She created an exercise that helps identify all aspects of a project, and provides a model for planning meetings. She believes in aggressive planning initially to avoid wasting time with corrective actions later.

Most projects are a series of interdependent events achieved in an orderly progression. A timeline listing goal dates, details for each stage and assigned persons, is essential.

The four keys to project management that will keep you focused include:

1. **Planning.** "Invite the most negative person, and the most positive person in your organization to help plan," McCleskey says. A negative person will scrutinize heavily, pointing out what can go wrong. While brainstorming, the positive person frequently offers creative answers.

2. **Assigning.** Determine what needs to be done, and who needs to do it. The best person is not just anyone. You may need to recruit people with special skills.

3. **Controlling.** This is not micro-management, but simply keeping people on track and on time with their assignments.

4. **Evaluating.** Don't wait until the project is complete. Evaluate periodically. Did you meet midpoint goals? If not, make adjustments. Is someone holding up progress? If so, take corrective action. Recognize those who are on target.

Take this quiz to assess your project management skills. Keeping in mind the four keys, number items you think should come first, second, third, etc. See solution at right. Use this model to plan your next project.

Source: Kathleen McCleskey, KM Consulting and Training Connection, Austin, TX.
Phone (512) 219-7058.
E-mail: kmccleskey@AOL.com

Content not available in this edition

Volunteer Training Primer: Principles, Procedures and Ideas for Training and Educating Volunteers.
Edited by Scott C. Stevenson.
© 2009 Stevenson, Inc. Published 2009 by Stevenson, Inc.

TRAINING RESOURCES & ENVIRONMENT

Position descriptions should be a must for any volunteer project. Handbooks also serve as a handy reference and help to avoid problems. And to invite their input and encourage them to gain greater ownership, you may find it extremely helpful to hold a once-a-year retreat for all your volunteers. Retreats represent the perfect time to establish goals and get everyone to look at the big picture.

Position Descriptions Should Point to the 'Big Picture'

It goes without saying that any volunteer position worth filling should include a written position description. Beyond that, however, each position description should include both specific job duties plus how those duties impact the work of the organization. No matter how menial the task may appear, including with its description implications of how it benefits the agency as a whole helps the volunteer to recognize the important ways he/she is contributing to the organization's goals and mission.

Below are two sample job duties and accompanying implications that might be found on a written position description.

Specific Job Duty:

- Enter volunteer data into our volunteer database.

Larger Implications:

a) Enables the agency to better serve volunteers who assist us.
b) Allows the agency to recruit and manage larger numbers of volunteers, and more volunteers means we're better able to serve those in need.
c) Allows paid staff to do a better job of managing.

Specific Job Duty:

- Schedule volunteer work days and times.

Larger Implications:

a) Helps volunteers identify scheduling that works best for them.
b) Allows the agency to expand the number of volunteers who can contribute time.
c) Ensures that adequate staff are on hand to meet the needs of those served by the agency.

Great Way to Write Training Information

Putting together a new training manual for your volunteers? Creating a brochure that describes what volunteering encompasses at your organization?

Here's a great way to make the writing go more smoothly: Meet with a potential volunteer who is unfamiliar with your agency or the topic you intend to write about.

Have a tape recorder handy. Tell the would-be volunteer that you would like him/her to consider volunteering for your cause. Then turn on your recorder, sit back and let the individual begin asking questions that come to mind. After each question, provide a detailed answer.

Your 10-minute conversation will provide the initial draft for a "Common Questions and Answers" section in your manual or brochure.

TRAINING RESOURCES & ENVIRONMENT

Well-organized Handbook Helps Avoid 'No One Told Me' Syndrome

Provide new volunteers with a well-organized handbook during orientation procedures.

According to Mary Kay Hood, director of volunteer services, Hendricks Community Hospital, (Danville, IN), and author of "The One Minute Answer to Volunteer Management Questions," "A handbook is a useful tool that outlines the basic work rules for your organization."

Though handbooks will vary depending on the nature of particular organizations and their services, Hood offers these standard topics for including in a volunteer handbook:

- Welcome letter
- Agency vision, mission, values
- Volunteer services department mission
- Reporting accidents/illnesses
- Safety plan in event of a disaster
- Uniform/appearance policy
- Corporate compliance policy

- How to become a volunteer
- Attendance/absence policy
- Signing in and out for duties
- Volunteer rights statement
- Harassment
- Benefits of being a volunteer
- Rights as a volunteer

Source: Mary Kay Hood, Director of Volunteer Services, Hendricks Community Hospital, Danville, IN. Phone (317) 745-4451.

Key Components for Position Descriptions

Some nonprofits make the mistake of classifying all volunteers under one job category and then varying their assignments and expectations. The result is volunteers not quite sure about what's expected of them.

Having a description for each volunteer position will eliminate that confusion. Be sure each description includes:

Job title — Avoid a general title such as office volunteer. Instead, come up with a specific and meaningful title, such as newsletter production member.

Date — The date the description was written or last updated to serve as a reminder to review the description occasionally and update it as needed.

Description summary — A one- or two-sentence description that captures the essence of the position.

Qualifications — Be as specific as necessary, including minimum qualifications, not ideal ones.

Job duties/activities — This is a list of specific tasks to be performed, perhaps categorized under like headings.

Working conditions — Indicate if the job involves hazardous conditions, outside or strenuous work, etc.

Conditions of service — Is reliable transportation necessary? Does the organization reimburse transportation and parking costs? Is a uniform provided? Are meals provided? Are there any other benefits or considerations that a volunteer should know about?

Supervision — Volunteers need to know who their immediate supervisors are and where those persons fit within the organization. Problems can quickly arise if a volunteer doesn't know who to approach with questions or from whom he/she should take direction.

How About Holding a Volunteer Camp?

Looking for some ways to put fun into volunteer training sessions? How about holding a fall volunteer camp — like the summer camps you remember attending as a kid?

Find a camp (church camp, YMCA, etc.) that has facilities you can use for a day, a weekend or even a week. (Some camps become more idle after the summer months.) Then build your training sessions around other more traditional camp activities — swimming, crafts, outdoor games, etc.

You might even be able to find a way of collaborating with camp officials to reduce or eliminate the cost of using their facilities.

In addition to holding training sessions, some of your fun activities may complement the training, such as scheduling team-building games for all attendees.

Fun Camp Activities

- ✓ Old-fashioned kid games (e.g., Red Rover, Red Rover)
- ✓ Ropes team-building exercise
- ✓ Sunrise yoga
- ✓ Wienie and marshmallow roasts
- ✓ Learning workshops: Identifying birds and trees, investing for retirement, etc.
- ✓ Campfire songs and scarey story telling

TRAINING RESOURCES & ENVIRONMENT

Write Multiple Position Descriptions

Should you write detailed position descriptions for every volunteer position you have?

Yes, says Kate Wanderer, volunteer services coordinator, Fairfax County Public Library (Fairfax, VA). From administrative assistant to gardener, library aide to scrapbooker, she says, she and her branch volunteer coordinators create a description for each volunteer position and posts them on the library's website for several reasons:

1. The library director encourages staff to involve volunteers in every aspect of the library.

2. Position descriptions provide a concrete basis for recruiting, training and evaluating volunteers.

3. Volunteers want to know what is expected of them and what else is available if they'd like a change of pace.

4. Visitors to the website and branches can see that the library makes a serious effort to enhance the efforts of paid staff for the benefit of customers.

5. Applicants can get a comprehensive idea about what volunteers do at the library, then fill out an online application that includes their special interests.

Source: Kate Wanderer, Volunteer Services Coordinator, Fairfax County Public Library, Fairfax, VA. Phone (703) 324-8332. E-mail: kate.wanderer@fairfaxcounty.gov

Content not available in this edition

TRAINING RESOURCES & ENVIRONMENT

Create Volunteer Handbook

Most essential ingredients for volunteer handbooks are the same, regardless of the duties your volunteers perform.

When Jamine Hamner, coordinator of volunteer services, Saint Joseph Healthcare (Lexington, KY), and her staff created a 33-page volunteer orientation handbook, they made sure to include all possible information their volunteers needed to know.

Hamner reviewed examples of other handbooks and used information from the "JCAHO Standards for Volunteer Departments" manual for her handbook, which is given to every volunteer at orientation to learn from and to keep as a guide for annual retesting.

The handbook, she says, "is an easy, concise way to get pertinent information to the volunteers. It gives them a reference book for future questions or concerns as well."

The handbook, which also allows Hamner to overlap written volunteer and Human Resources policies in a form all volunteers can access, is posted online at: www.saintjosephhealthcare.org/pdf/VolunteerOrientationHandbook.pdf

Source: Jamine Hamner, Coordinator of Volunteer Services, Saint Joseph HealthCare, Lexington, KY. Phone (859) 813-1290. E-mail: hamnerja@sjhlex.org

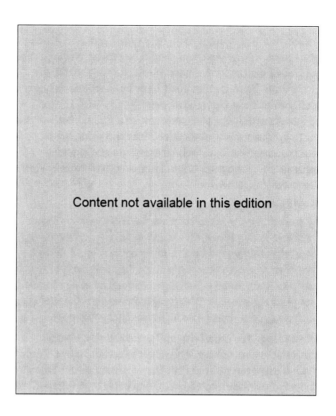
Content not available in this edition

Use of Training CD Beneficial to Volunteers

With more than 900 people volunteering at St. Luke's Hospital (Bethlehem, PA) a year, the hospital's volunteer services office wanted to create a training tool that would be innovative and cost effective.

Georgina Winfield, volunteer services coordinator, took the lead, with the assistance of co-workers, on the project and developed a CD orientation that allows the volunteers the flexibility of reviewing the information in the comfort of their homes. Winfield says to date she has spent 40 hours producing 400 CDs at a cost of approximately $270.

Now, instead of the previous two-hour, in-person orientation, the orientation can be completed within an hour. Then the volunteer must attend a half-hour review session where a post-test is administered. To date, more than 350 people have used the CD.

"We have a tremendous amount of volunteers and interns and we needed to look at an innovative and cost effective way to provide all with an adequate and consistent orientation, without needing to take up a large portion of our busy schedules," she says.

The CD was created using a program called Swishmax, which is similar to a flash media program or a website. Winfield says it was designed so the program would be user-friendly, fun and visually appealing.

"The CD is set up to automatically start once inserted into the computer. Individuals are to read the information on the screen and then press the 'next' button. There are also 'back' and 'main menu' buttons so people can move freely throughout the orientation," she says.

"It is not a bunch of PDF files on a computer page instead of a book," says Winfield. "Each page begins with special effects in various colors. A variety of pictures and other images were also incorporated to make it eye catching and fun. There are also series of pictures that demonstrate how to do specific things."

Winfield says the new CD enforces different learning methods for each volunteer. "Everyone learns in various ways and those methods are incorporated throughout the entire orientation process. Audibly — hearing the information previously read at the orientation; visually — viewing/reading the orientation CD; and experientially — performing certain tasks at the orientation."

Source: Georgina Winfield, Volunteer Services Coordinator, St. Luke's Hospital, Bethlehem, PA. Phone (610) 954-4676. E-mail: winfieg@slhn.org

TRAINING RESOURCES & ENVIRONMENT

Retreat Planning for Volunteers

Asking your key volunteers to take time from their schedules for a retreat means the event should be productive, enjoyable and free of distractions. Those involved should leave the retreat with the sense that goals have been set and stronger relationships have been developed.

First, determine the primary purpose of the retreat, whether it is to brainstorm about creative ideas and solutions for your organization, or to build friendships and enhance camaraderie. Following are additional options to help you plan a fruitful gathering:

Decide how long the retreat will be. Some volunteers may enjoy spending a weekend at a nearby lodge, park or resort. If distance isn't a factor, they won't need to spend the night, but arrange for them to be able to reserve a room if desired. Choose an area with other attractions they may wish to see on their own time. Make effective use of hotel meeting rooms for your planning sessions. Plan meals so everyone dines together. Being away from home also helps minimize disruptions.

Set the stage for creativity and productivity. Plan a comfortable atmosphere and encourage casual attire, keeping in mind that even morning or afternoon retreats are longer than a typical meeting. Choose a place that's private and well equipped with all necessary supplies, and have a variety of food and beverages close at hand.

Reserve the nicest area of your own facility. Your institution may have the meeting rooms, food service, office equipment and supplies you need, making it impractical for your retreat to be held away. However, try an "upgrade" from your usual meeting place, such as an auditorium or boardroom. Request better china for coffee and lunch, and a full hot meal rather than the usual coffee and rolls. The more formal setting will help those attending get in a businesslike state of mind, as well as show them that you consider them to be important.

Try an outdoor picnic, sports or cultural event. If you usually meet in a formal, no-nonsense setting, have a catered picnic in a botanical garden pavilion, or reserve the conference room of your local zoo, country club or museum.

After the meeting, the reward can be a festive boxed lunch and enjoying the nearby attractions. Remember that those who may not find common ground in your organization may connect in a friendly way on the tennis or golf court, or while viewing artwork or animals.

Keep the agenda on track, but build in flexibility. Wherever your group meets, cover all necessary topics and goals thoroughly, but leave room for other matters. Having your key volunteers in the same place at the same time is certain to result in discussion of important ideas that have not yet been openly aired.

Ask volunteers what type of retreat they want to attend. Be open-minded to excursions like out-of-town shopping trips on a chartered bus, or a family trip to a sports event. Even if little business is accomplished, your volunteers will certainly be discussing goals and dreams for your institution's benefit. Providing a social setting away from the usual environment gives those who have never had a chance to become acquainted during routine volunteer tasks the perfect excuse to learn more about each other.

Ask the right planning questions to maximize retreat results....

- What is the primary purpose of the retreat — training, planning, recognition of achievements/ contributions?
- Are there secondary objectives? What are they?
- What level of interaction will I want at the retreat?
- Would it be helpful to hire an outside facilitator?
- What can be done to maximize attendance?
- What printed materials/handouts will be essential?
- What needs to happen so participants will leave feeling enthused and motivated?
- What surprises might be interjected to hold audience attention?

Help Volunteers Realize Challenging, Achievable Goals

As you know, people are motivated for different reasons. Nevertheless, most individuals are gratified when they make achievements. That's why it makes sense to look at every volunteer-related program (e.g., training and retreats) you have and determine what can be done to make it more goal oriented.

As you examine each program, keep these achievement principles in mind:

- Goals should be challenging but realistic.
- In addition to an overall goal, include intermediate goals along the way.
- Remember to include appropriate incentives and/or

celebrations with corresponding achievements.
- Identify a variety of achievement goal types — those for individuals as well as groups. This helps everyone have an opportunity to accomplish something.
- Allow volunteers input in determining challenging but achievable goals.
- Once goals have been set, be sure to monitor progress through regular meetings, updates in correspondence and other ways.

People enjoy winning causes, so do what you can to help them win along the way.

TRAINING RESOURCES & ENVIRONMENT

Ingredients for Worthwhile Retreats

Retreats often serve as very useful planning or strategizing opportunities for board members and/or volunteers.

If you want board members or volunteers to keep coming back to retreats — or even participate in one as a newcomer — it's important they believe their time is being well spent.

Here are ways to make your next retreat a positive experience for its participants:

- **Plan and organize your retreat thoroughly.** A well-thought-out agenda will demonstrate to participants that you mean business and also respect their time. Stick to your timeline.

- **Enlist a competent facilitator and/or moderator.** The person leading the retreat should keep attendees enthusiastic and participatory.

- **Get participants talking early on.** The surest way to put everyone to sleep is to lecture to them. Instead, seek audience input and discussion of key issues.

- **Treat all ideas and opinions with respect.** Make it clear, up front, that no idea is a bad idea. Encourage all participants to remember the golden rule as they work to plan and resolve issues.

- **Make the experience motivating.** Help participants become and remain enthused. Incorporate a brief talk from an exciting speaker. Develop goals and objectives that participants can become excited about.

- **Don't forget to make it "fun."** Although participants should leave knowing a great deal was accomplished, the experience should also be uplifting. Provide time for socializing, rewarding attendees when appropriate and incorporating strategies that help people to smile.

While a poorly executed retreat will make it next to impossible to attract future attendees, a productive retreat will serve as a fulfilling and motivating experience and will ensure repeat participation in future events as well.

Gear Presentations to the Age of Your Audience

Depending on the age group that you're training, you may want to evaluate your presentation and handouts by first taking into consideration the needs of your audience. Consider the following:

Mature adult volunteers — Consider revising your materials and presentation to allow for those who may have vision or hearing problems. Create handouts with larger type for ease of reading and speak more slowly and louder. However, don't assume that all seniors need accommodations such as large-print handouts. Be sure to ask the group who would like these altered presentation materials and offer regular handouts to the others as not to offend anyone. When adjusting your speaking volume, ask the participants at the outset whether the volume of your voice is easy to hear and then adjust accordingly.

Youth volunteers — Keep the pace of your presentation lively to engage this group of volunteers. Add music to the presentation and be sure to keep the interaction and exchanges lively. Use visual aids that offer concise bullet points and graphics that will engross the youthful audience. Don't forget to ask for their specific ideas for ways in which they best serve the organization to offer a sense of ownership to these volunteers.

Mid-aged volunteers — This group is extraordinarily busy with all the demands on their lives from career to kids. Make the presentation concise, clear and create handouts that can be reviewed at home. Be sure to include contact information — especially an e-mail address — so these volunteers can contact you for more details or clarifications after the training. Purposefully cut the presentation time by 10 to 15 minutes so your audience will be pleasantly surprised by your concise delivery.

Honing your next presentation to the age of your audience will most effectively allow you to present your message in a way that not only engages your audience, but also tailors it to the audience members' needs.

Role Playing
Provides Valuable Learning Experience

Do you incorporate role playing into training workshops? It can offer a valuable way to teach through play acting.

Here are some ideas to make your role-playing sessions more effective:

- Have participants act out situations that have actually happened in previous years as a way to learn how to handle the unexpected.

- Have trainees critique each other's role-playing and offer improvements.

- Look to your constituency to find those who have experience in training. Then have them conduct the sessions.

Volunteer Training Primer: Principles, Procedures and Ideas for Training and Educating Volunteers.
Edited by Scott C. Stevenson.
© 2009 Stevenson, Inc. Published 2009 by Stevenson, Inc.

15 TEACHING & TRAINING TECHNIQUES

There are dozens of different training techniques you can use to teach and educate your volunteers. Some of the examples shown here include using visualization, storytelling, an exercise that uses hats, journaling and much more. Make use of multiple techniques to get valuable skills instilled.

When to Include Shadowing as Part of Volunteer Training

How do you know if you should include shadowing as part of training new volunteers? It depends on the position. If the position is hard to learn without having hands-on experience, you may want to enlist an experienced volunteer to help with training.

For example, Lisa Shuman, coordinator of volunteers, Harrison Memorial Animal Hospital (Denver, CO), says monitoring is the most intense, hands-on position they have. These volunteers help with pre- and post-spaying and neutering procedures. Their duties rely heavily on the medical side: extubating patients; cleaning incision areas; and watching for problems (e.g., dropping heart rates).

Since the majority of volunteers recruited don't have a background in veterinary medicine, hands-on training is essential. Every volunteer new to this position must shadow an experienced volunteer for at least three shifts. Each shift is four and a half hours long and the volunteers work side-by-side during the shadowing.

Shuman says having the new volunteers shadow an experienced volunteer has more benefits than just making sure they receive adequate training. The senior volunteers are a point of contact for Shuman, giving her feedback about the training and the new volunteer. The senior volunteer can tell her if the new volunteer is right for the fast-paced position or if more training is required. "They (senior volunteers) are the right people to do the training. They know what to look for in a new volunteer," says Shuman.

Source: Lisa Shuman, Coordinator of Volunteers, Harrison Memorial Animal Hospital, Denver, CO. Phone (303) 722-2100. E-mail: lshuman@hmah.org

'Buzz Groups' Promote Exchange of Ideas

If you're training a large group of volunteers, make use of buzz group sessions to break the monotony and foster learning among your participants.

Here's how it works: Divide participants into small groups that meet for a short time, usually as part of a longer training session. The group considers a simple question or problem, offering ideas and solutions. Ideas from each smaller group are then presented to the total group to promote further discussion.

Buzz groups are different than brainstorming because they generally emphasize problem solving.

> Buzz groups are particularly helpful:
>
> ✓ When the group is too large for everyone to participate.
> ✓ When studying more complex subjects.
> ✓ When time is limited.

Prizes Get Volunteers to Attend Trainings

When volunteer positions require intensive, ongoing training, it might be difficult to get volunteers to always attend.

That's why Rita Lawson, Client Services, Life Choices Medical Clinic and Resource Center (Joplin, MO), awards her crisis counselor volunteers with prizes at the end of each two-hour quarterly continuing education classes.

Lawson likes to conclude the training sessions with fun because they are very intensive with a structured agenda. At the end of the training door prizes are drawn for volunteers. Lawson likes to tie the prizes into a theme. For example, items with a Fourth of July theme were given away at the June training.

There are also extra awards for every volunteer who has perfect attendance for all of the trainings. These are bigger prizes — $100 gift certificates to the local mall. She says she usually has 80 percent of her 25 to 30 volunteer attend all of the trainings.

"I make it clear that they should think of their volunteer position like a job. This is serious work," she says.

The volunteer manual states that crisis counselor volunteers must attend all of the trainings, but they are allowed one emergency absence.

Source: Rita Lawson, Client Services, Life Choices Medical Clinic and Resource Center, Joplin, MO. Phone (417) 623-0131. E-mail: rital@lifechoices4states.org

15 TEACHING & TRAINING TECHNIQUES

Use Visualization To Help Educate Volunteers

Whether in formal training or while volunteers are performing their jobs, help them develop a greater appreciation for their work by visualizing the outcome of their efforts.

Explain what completed work will help to accomplish in addressing your nonprofit's mission. How do their jobs fit into the larger picture? Help them to realize that, what may appear to be a menial task positively impacts those you serve.

Paint a picture of how their work will make a noticeable difference.

Tip to Reinforce Training

You've heard of a suggestion box, but how about a competency box?

Heather Powers, volunteer coordinator, Condell Medical Center Hospice (Libertyville, IL), uses a competency box at roundtable meetings with volunteers. The box is filled with questions based on volunteer continuing education training as well as situational problems.

During the meetings, a volunteer pulls out a question and tries to answer it in front of the group. Powers says it's a great way to engage volunteers, offer praise for right answers and correct misconceptions.

Heather Powers, Volunteer Coordinator, Condell Medical Center Hospice, Libertyville, IL. Phone (847) 573-4059. E-mail: hpowers@condell.org

Incorporate Puzzles Into Your Next Training Session

Ever considered including crossword puzzles or word jumbles into your next volunteer training session?

With more than 30 years of volunteer training experience, Terrie Temkin, founding principal, CoreStrategies for Nonprofits (Miami, FL), has perfected the way she presents materials to volunteers by including puzzles in the training.

"I try to think about how to get information across without being just a talking head," she says. "I'm a strong believer that when people actively do things, they learn better than when they just sit and listen. With that philosophy, I have to come up with different ways to present the material."

Before creating the puzzles, Temkin meets with the organization and at least three training participants to identify the training session's goals.

Temkin then creates an outline that features techniques she feels will best help her audience reach those objectives. Depending on the group's needs, Temkin incorporates puzzles with games, lectures, group discussions or brainstorming — always making sure to process the exercises to ensure participants walk away with a firm grasp of critical information.

"I try to build puzzles that assess where they're already at, what they already know and make clear what they still need to learn," she says. Temkin's puzzles have been created from scratch as well as from computer software programs.

Once in the training session, the puzzle exercises are approached with a "unite and conquer" attitude, with the volunteers working at the puzzles in groups.

"I like to keep the groups relatively small because anything more than six people and you tend to have one person take over and leave the others not as involved."

Source: Terrie Temkin, Founding Principal, CoreStrategies for Nonprofits, Miami, FL. Phone (888) 458-4351, ext. 3. E-mail: terrietemkin@corestrategies4nonprofits.com

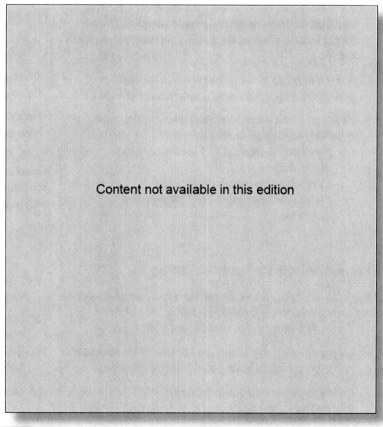

Content not available in this edition

15 TEACHING & TRAINING TECHNIQUES

Bring in Creative Themes to Make Trainings Fun

Give your next volunteer training session a theme.

In doing so, you'll most likely get more volunteers to attend, give volunteers a chance to network with each other and create a relaxed atmosphere for volunteers to speak honestly about your program.

Case in point: Debi Wagner is currently volunteer coordinator for Catholic Charities (Oklahoma City, OK). At a previous position as director of the America Reads Program for RSVP of Central Oklahoma, Wagner says, she needed to get feedback from volunteers about how new training materials were working for a volunteer tutoring program.

So she decided to have some fun with the training and threw a "Learning Luau."

In picking a fun theme, Wagner says, she wanted to reach beyond the core group of volunteers who usually attend the trainings. Without a huge budget, an inexpensive "luau" was easy to throw.

The 20 or so volunteers who attended the training enjoyed (unlit) tiki torches, a buffet of Hawaiian foods and,

if they wore luau-themed clothing, RSVP promotional prizes such as T-shirts and mugs.

The approach worked, she says, noting that the Hawaiian-themed event drew the usual dependable attendees, as well as several volunteers who normally don't attend such meetings.

Volunteers grazed the buffet table and ate while Wagner covered her agenda, having her volunteers share experiences, challenges and frustrations about the new material they were using in a comfortable and fun environment.

While the "Learning Luau" was Wagner's first fun themed training session, she says she always tries to incorporate a fun and friendly environment into every volunteer event. She makes good use of agency promotional items for giveaways, gives her volunteers holiday gifts and makes up trivia questions for icebreakers.

Source: Debi Wagner, Volunteer Coordinator, Catholic Charities, Oklahoma City, OK. Phone (405) 523-3000. E-mail: dwagner@catholiccharities.ok.org

Get Your Group to Affirm One Another's Strengths

If you have a relatively small group of volunteers who know one another, here's an exercise designed to strengthen synergy among them:

1. Hand out index cards to each person, giving one card less than the total number of people attending (for example, in a group of six, you'd give each person five cards).

2. Ask participants to write the names of the persons present on their index cards — one name per card.

3. Next, ask participants to write answers to the following questions on each of their index cards:
   - Name one or more of this individual's most admired traits.
   - This is the first person I would turn to if....
   - I wish I could be more like [Name] when it comes to....

Allow a few minutes for everyone to complete responses on the cards. Then, choosing one participant at a time, have others read how they described that person. Spend time discussing that individual's strengths before moving on to the next person.

> **Melissa Evans**
>
> Most admired traits:
> Patience, sense of humor, baking skills, creativity
>
> She's the first person I'd turn to if
> I needed a great batch of cookies on short notice
>
> I wish I could be more like her when it comes to:
> Coordinating big events and talking others into helping, like for our annual bake sale! She makes it better (and more profitable) every year!

Use Modeling to Train Volunteers

People do what people see. One of the most effective ways to train new volunteers is through modeling.

Try these modeling tips to train new volunteers:

✓ Select a model who is liked and respected by volunteers and is perceived as having credibility or expertise.

✓ Volunteers should do more than passively observe the model. Have them take notes or imagine themselves

carrying out various tasks demonstrated by the model.

✓ Have the model indicate the likely consequences of carrying out the behavior effectively. For example, show the model receiving positive feedback for appropriate behavior.

✓ Gradually fade out the model rather than abruptly terminating the relationship.

15 TEACHING & TRAINING TECHNIQUES

Pass Out Questions, Discuss Answers

Whether you are educating a small group of volunteers or training other staff, try using the "Q & A method" of involving your group's participants in the learning process.

Come up with a list of key questions your presentation is intended to answer, then list those questions on separate pieces of paper and distribute them in sealed and numbered envelopes to each of your attendees.

Ask whoever has envelope No. 1 to open it and read his/her question aloud. Then spend the next few minutes discussing possible answers as a group. Use the same procedure for the remaining envelopes and questions.

This teaching method serves to involve participants more than would simply speaking to the group. They become more aware of key questions about the topic at hand and also help in shaping answers to these questions.

Break Up Training With a Massage

While working on a big project, or sitting through a long training session, try this simple relaxation exercise.

1. Ask everyone to stand and form a line, shoulder to shoulder. Now, have everyone turn one-quarter so each person is looking at another person's back.

2. At the count of three, everyone places their hands on the shoulders of the person in front of them and massages the neck and shoulders of that person until you announce, "Stop!"

3. Now, instruct everyone to turn and face in the opposite direction and repeat the exercise. Conclude the break by asking everyone to turn to the people on both sides and say "thank you."

Incorporate 'Hats' Into Your Workshop

If you conduct volunteer workshops, training sessions or other group events from time to time, you're no doubt looking for ways to make presentations more interesting for participants. One way to do that is with the use of hats.

Collect an array of different types of hats and caps you can use either at the beginning of your workshop or throughout the entire presentation to convey key messages to your attendees (see ideas at right). The hats add an element of fun to the presentation and also help emphasize certain points. Donning a different hat from time to time breaks up the monotony and takes the "lecturing" out of what might otherwise be a boring experience.

You may even choose a more interactive approach and ask audience members to wear one of your hats as a way to involve them in the workshop.

And who knows — you may have a volunteer who has an interest in hat lore or a collection of unusual head gear who can help you with the planning.

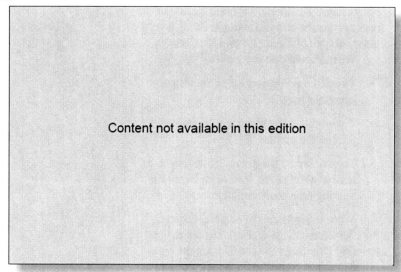

Content not available in this edition

Storytelling Teaches and Transforms

Next time you need to get a lesson across to board members or volunteers, don't underestimate the power of storytelling as a way in inform and enlighten them.

Stories provide a wonderful way of conveying information. They bring out the attentive child in each of us.

Try incorporating any of these storytelling methods into your next presentation as a way of conveying a particular point:

- Invite a child to come and read a particular passage or story. It can be powerful.
- Locate someone with storytelling experience to perform during your session.

- If your group is relatively small, begin a story appropriate for the session, then go around the room, asking each participant to add to the story.
- Share a "what if" story with your volunteers: What if our agency received a $5 million gift.... or what if we had no volunteers available to help?
- Begin your meeting by sharing the first portion of a story, then stop at a point that keeps your group wondering how it will end. Save the end of your story as the last item on your meeting's agenda.

15 TEACHING & TRAINING TECHNIQUES

Let's Make a Deal: Utilizing Games in Volunteer Training Programs

Games can do many things to make training a better experience for staff or volunteers. They're fun, they break the ice, reinforce learning, are nonthreatening and can be a great way to introduce people, pique their interest and reinforce principles, concepts and techniques covered in training.

Training doesn't have to be boring, and games provide the opportunity for an interactive training format that allows people to work in teams and use humor to learn about a topic, say Suzanne McCormick, vice president of agency services, United Way of Greater Portland (Portland, ME), and Barbara Wentworth, community services director, United Way of York County (Kennebunk, ME).

Games also provide an action-oriented, interactive, experience-based type of training that includes the group, not just the individual, and creates active involvement and participation, instead of a passive, formal type of training. "The trainer takes on the role of the resource person and facilitator, creating a very informal type of training," says McCormick.

When should you use games?

- **To open a program.** It sets the tone and energizes people.

- **Throughout the program.** It changes the pace of the training.

- **To conclude a program.** It allows you to review what's been learned and ends the training on a positive note.

When using games in training, however, says McCormick, make them relevant to the training: "You need to base them on the type of information or the type of training you're trying to provide." Also, provide incentives, even if they're just a piece of candy or a pencil.

Sources: Suzanne McCormick, Vice President of Agency Services, United Way of Greater Portland, Portland, ME. Phone (207) 874-1000.
E-mail: smccormick@unitedwaygp.org
Barbara Wentworth, Community Services Director, United Way of York County, Kennebunk, ME.
Phone (207) 985-3359. E-mail: uwycme@uwycme.org

Content not available in this edition

15 TEACHING & TRAINING TECHNIQUES

Journaling Serves as Effective Training Tool

Have you ever considered using journaling as a method of on-the-job training?

Mary Forti, volunteer coordinator, Women's Resource Center of the New River Valley (Radford, VA), says journal writing is one of the requirements its crisis intervention volunteers go through during their 15 hours of on-the-job training.

"It's part of the overall supervision plan," Forti says. "Because I am not directly supervising each person during the on-the-job training process, each journal keeps me apprised of each volunteer's progress, concerns and issues I need to address.

"The journals also have a therapeutic value for the volunteers," she adds. "The act of writing itself helps to clarify concerns, process feelings and helps the volunteer individual track progress."

Each journal entry answers three questions:

1. **What I did during my shift.** This gives Forti a sense of what each volunteer is accomplishing and what kind of follow-up she may need to provide.

2. **How I felt during my shift.** This helps the volunteer see the importance of his/her emotions while serving in the helping role and develop a greater sense of objectivity when dealing with difficult events and individuals. Answers may also indicate if a volunteer may be heading for burnout or losing him/herself in the work.

3. **Questions I have or observations/reflections.** "When we do the volunteer's final interview (as part of our certification process), we use these as a springboard for discussion/clarification," says Forti. She notes that because the questions are usually tied to a specific situation or event, there's plenty of room for dialogue.

Forti does not impose any time requirements for journal entries but does ask volunteers to write journals entries closely timed to the end of each shift so thoughts, questions and concerns are still fresh. She also asks that the volunteer's journal writing takes place off site to get a little emotional distance and benefit from a quieter setting.

Source: Mary Forti, Volunteer Coordinator, Women's Resource Center of the New River Valley, Radford, VA. Phone (540) 639-1123. E-mail: volunteers@wrcnrv.org

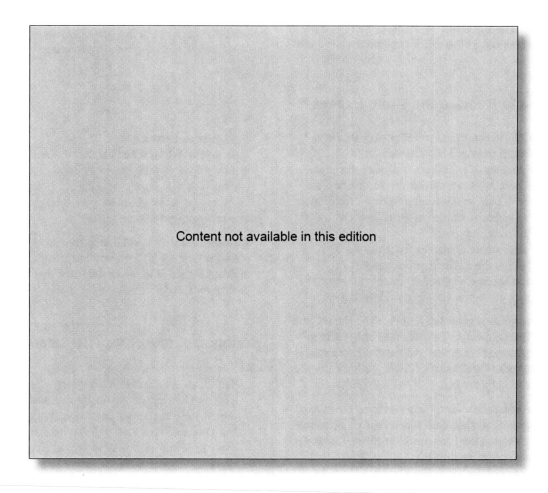

Content not available in this edition

Volunteer Training Primer: Principles, Procedures and Ideas for Training and Educating Volunteers.
Edited by Scott C. Stevenson.
© 2009 Stevenson, Inc. Published 2009 by Stevenson, Inc.

NURTURING LEADERS

How do you turn an everyday volunteer into a leader? Are those skills innate, or can they be taught? How do you go about bringing out someone's leadership skills? What can you do to move people to higher levels of service?

Nurture Leadership Skills in Volunteers

Your next board president or event chair may be right under your nose.

In seeking to nurture your volunteers into more responsibility, realize that some people are born leaders, others have no desire for leadership, and still others may just need some guidance and training to become great leaders.

Cofounders of Hands On Greater Richmond (Richmond, VA), Vanessa Diamond, Kristen Kaplan and Elaine Summerfield recruit and train volunteers to be team leaders. Training is based on skills Diamond used to develop leaders with AmeriCorps.

Diamond says some persons simply volunteer to be team leaders, while others are referred by their team leaders and need to be asked. To help instill leadership in persons who may not see potential within themselves, she asks them in a way that empowers them, gives them both control and support in the leadership process and gradually increases responsibilities until they are comfortable to take on a higher role.

Rather than put out a mass call for volunteers — which

Diamond says leads to few, if any leads — she makes the contact personal, telling a prospect she believes he/she would be a great leader and sharing how his/her volunteer work can help the organization. With this method, Diamond says she is rarely turned down.

Persons who agree to become leaders undergo training and receive constant support, including what Hands On's expectations are. Diamond says they give leaders the right tools to accomplish their tasks, but let them choose how to use the tools.

While some volunteers just might not be ready to take on leadership positions with huge responsibilities, such as serving on a board, Diamond says she and her colleagues build volunteers up for major leadership roles by first giving them smaller leadership opportunities and promoting them higher and higher.

Source: Vanessa Diamond, Cofounder, Hands On Greater Richmond, Richmond, VA. Phone (804) 330-7400.
E-mail: volunteer@handsongreaterrichmond.org

If You Hope to Receive the Most, Expect It

It's often said, "We become products of our environment," and there is so much truth in that statement.

If our expectations of volunteers and board members are moderate at best, moderate performance is the best we will ever receive. If paid staff exhibit mediocre commitment toward their jobs and achievement of goals, how can we expect volunteers to do anymore?

Create an atmosphere of high expectations for volunteers and watch them "rise to the occasion."

To help them become all that they can be, incorporate these management principles into your work with them:

- **Show them what is expected of them.** You should have clearly defined objectives for individual volunteers as well as structured committees and boards. This includes job descriptions as well as quantifiable goals for the year or the duration of a project.

- **Enlist one or two leaders** to help you bring the others to a new level of performance. Share your expectations with those who can help you motivate others. Ask them to focus their efforts on this task.

- **Recognize and reward** those who are living up to expectations. Whenever a volunteer demonstrates behavior that lives up to your highest expectations, recognize him/her both individually and publicly. Consider offering incentives for those who meet incremental benchmarks as they progress toward stated goals.

- **Include volunteers and board members** in the planning process. If you want these people to "own" a higher standard of involvement, they should be involved in shaping and determining objectives.

Recognize How Rare True Leaders Are

■ The ability to lead others is a rare quality and one that should not be dismissed easily. When you have a volunteer that possesses this quality, it is important to encourage and empower them. Support from you and your staff will inspire them to do everything in their power to help achieve your organizational goals.

NURTURING LEADERS

Train Volunteers to Work With Support Groups

Consider using a step-by-step approach when training volunteers for a support group leadership role.

Jackie Frederiksen, program manager, National Multiple Sclerosis Society, North Central States (Sioux Falls, SD), says she takes a three-step approach for training volunteers to become self-help group leaders.

First, the volunteer is brought into the office to get an overview of the position. Frederiksen says they explain the self-help leader's responsibilities and time commitment required. All self-help leaders are required to give a one-year commitment for the groups' monthly meetings. Because the position requires dedication and responsibility, volunteers are given time to decide if they accept the task.

The next step is to give the self-help leader a detailed training manual developed by the national office. Frederiksen says the manual covers every situation that could occur during a meeting and how it should be handled.

Volunteers then choose to visit a chapter office or participate in a conference call to discuss questions with staff. Frederiksen says this is important because the volunteer needs to feel comfortable with the position before they start.

Not only can staff answer questions about the manual, but they can also run situational training with the volunteer to clarify any situation that may occur.

Frederiksen says they look for the following in a self-help leader:

1. Experience dealing with MS, either as someone who has it, or someone who is a caregiver of a person with MS, so they can relate to the group members.

2. A person who has a prior relationship with the chapter. Frederiksen says it's important to pick someone they trust, because they are an extension of the chapter.

3. High-level volunteers who are dedicated, motivated and responsible.

4. Volunteers who are empathetic and have good listening skills.

Source: Jackie Frederiksen, Program Manager, National Multiple Sclerosis Society, North Central States, Sioux Falls, SD. Phone (605) 336-7017. E-mail: Jackie.frederiksen@nmss.org

Training Procedures Should Elevate Recruit Level to Level

Do your training procedures include an "on-the-job training" component that moves new volunteers from beginner level procedures to increasingly more advanced levels?

If getting thoroughly acclimated to your organization and/or programs requires higher levels of volunteer skills, explore an on-the-job training procedure that moves volunteers to increasingly more advanced levels of know-how. This step-by-step scenario will help to illustrate how it might work:

1. Begin by having new volunteers shadowing an experienced staff person or volunteer for an "observation only" period of hours or days.

2. Place the volunteer in a direct supervision setting that includes a staff person or trained volunteer providing detailed instructions as the new recruit begins his/her "learning by doing" procedure.

3. Lessen the direct supervision as the volunteer becomes more familiar with duties and procedures, but offer easy access to a staff person or trained volunteer should questions or problems arise.

4. By this stage, the volunteer is fully trained and doing his/her job with minimal supervision but is not prepared to teach others.

5. The final phase of volunteer competency includes additional procedures on how to train others. This represents the top level of volunteer know-how.

If your organization has jobs that require high levels of skill, you might want to evaluate the appropriateness of a procedure such as this. In addition to the advanced levels of on-the-job training, consider how you might make each increasingly skilled level carry with it a greater level of prestige and accompanying benefits.

Traits of a Volunteer Leader

Do you question which volunteers in your organization possess the skills necessary to be an effective leader? Here are some skills to look for in your volunteers to help identify a leader within your corp of volunteers:

- ❑ Ability to inspire others
- ❑ Ability to lead others
- ❑ Ability to follow through
- ❑ Ability to envision
- ❑ Ability to plan and organize
- ❑ Ability to motivate and mobilize
- ❑ Ability to manage
- ❑ Ability to communicate
- ❑ Ability to facilitate
- ❑ Ability to mentor
- ❑ Ability of make effective decisions
- ❑ Ability to collaborate

NURTURING LEADERS

14 Tips for New Volunteer Leaders

You've just been put in charge of a project or organization. Now what?

Kathleen McCleskey, KM Consulting & Training Connection (Liberty Hill, TX), has some questions you need to ask yourself. The answers will help guide you through the process of being a new leader.

1. **What's the project's purpose?** — "You've got to find out what the mission is. Why do we come in here as volunteers and do what we do?"

2. **Is there a strategic plan in place?** — "Some nonprofits have one and some do not. If there is one, is the project fitting into the strategic plan? A lot of times people go off on wonderful projects, but those projects are not a part of the strategic plan. You need a strategic plan to keep focused on what you're doing."

3. **Who is doing what job? How effectively?** — "Is there a board in place? Who are the other members on staff? Have volunteers been used effectively? You need to know these things to get a handle on what's going on within the organization."

4. **What are the established priorities?** — "Depending on how the organization is set up, maybe the board has set priorities or maybe the executive director has set those priorities, but you need to know that as a new leader."

5. **How do people communicate with each other — phone, newsletter, e-mail, fax?** — "Especially if you're working with a board or executive director, you need to ask, 'Do you want me to talk to you face-to-face, through e-mails, over the phone?' Is there a newsletter that goes out to volunteers or those who donate to the nonprofit?"

6. **What is the team's personality?** — "Are people laid back? Are there people who are very strategic in their thinking? You need to understand that to know who to go to in order to grow the program."

7. **With whom will you be interacting during projects?** — "Sometimes a nonprofit may have two or three missions and they all want volunteers. You'll have to build coalitions with those two or three missions."

8. **What documents, policies, etc., should you read to get you up to date and keep you up to date?** — "You need to build the groundwork with all the past policies and procedures before you begin."

9. **Are there any skeletons in the closet?** — "You need to know things like, was there a volunteer program here before that failed?" And if so, why?

10. **Are there any notes about previous meetings or after action reports about the project?** — "You need to look at every record of the project."

11. **Have the volunteers had any training? If so, what?** — "How much training do they need and do they need refresher training? What training do they need to be more beneficial to the nonprofit?"

12. **What activities have the volunteers participated in the past?** — "Some nonprofits have limits within the areas they'll allow volunteers to work. Let's look at the places they've worked and maybe see if we can build some others."

13. **What problems have been encountered in the past?** — "You need to look at volunteer-staff relationships. Are volunteers showing up on time?"

14. **Where is the historical knowledge?** — "Is it in a database somewhere? A folder? Or somebody's head? History can be people who have been on the board before or projects or articles written about the organization."

Source: Kathleen McCleskey, KM Consulting & Training Connection, Liberty, TX. Phone (512) 219-7058. E-mail: kmccleskey@aol.com

Content not available in this edition

NURTURING LEADERS

Nurture Junior Volunteers, Create Volunteers for Life

Even the youngest volunteer can make a difference, says Sherry Hodnett, volunteer and bereavement coordinator, Home Hospice of West Texas (Big Spring, TX), who started the Hospice Halos youth volunteer program three years ago.

Hospice Halos are volunteers age 11 to 14 who assist Hodnett once a week in serving hospice clients. They serve food, read to residents, call bingo, give manicures, help with events and bring roses to families of patients who have died.

Hodnett recommends these steps to create your junior volunteer program:

1. **Spread the word** to volunteers that you're starting a new program and would like to involve their children, grandchildren, nieces and nephews.

2. **Host an orientation meeting** to discuss expectations with volunteers and parents. Share a list of expected tasks so there are no surprises. Have volunteer and parent sign a letter stating they are expected to volunteer one day a week, plus waivers or confidentiality forms. Be specific on policies for cell phones, iPods, etc. Give parents infor-

mation to reach children during volunteer shifts.

3. **Provide complete training and/or in-services needed to begin volunteering.** This includes any tests or screenings, such as tuberculosis tests.

4. **Begin activities under supervision.** Provide and require volunteers to wear T-shirts or badges that identify them as volunteers.

5. **Add youth volunteers to your mailing lists** so they and their parents receive the latest newsletters or correspondence to stay informed on upcoming events and activities.

6. **At the end of the program or at your annual recognition event, reward youth volunteers** with positive feedback, certificates or a field trip to thank them for their participation. Have the volunteers complete a letter of interest to participate in the program in the upcoming year.

Source: Sherry Hodnett, Volunteer and Bereavement Coordinator, Home Hospice of West Texas, Big Spring, TX. Phone (432) 264-7599. E-mail: bshodnett@hotmail.com

Tips for Training Volunteer Supervisors

Properly training volunteers to supervise other volunteers can pay off in many ways. The first step is identifying potential candidates.

Wendy Bauer, volunteer coordinator, San Diego Asian American Repertory Theatre (San Diego, CA), oversees training for her organization's volunteers.

"Individuals who get along well with others, who have good organizational and leadership skills, who encourage others and demonstrate a desire to help others achieve their fullest potential or utilize their talents are ready to take on this responsibility," says Bauer.

But before they take on that responsibility, Bauer says, proper and thorough training is a must.

"The more you can expose them to the world of volunteerism and all the resources available to help them grow as leaders in this realm, the better," she says.

To accomplish this, Bauer says, potential volunteer supervisors should:

- attend workshops and training sessions about recruiting and working with volunteers,

- visit with other volunteers supervisors, and

- gradually work up to a supervisory role.

Bauer recommends providing opportunities for the potential supervisor to work with other volunteers in a leadership capacity. As they progress, increase their responsibility.

Once trained, Bauer says the benefits of volunteers

supervising volunteers are great: "They can closely relate to situations and circumstances a volunteer might find themselves in, and they come in with an energy driven by a desire to make the world a better place."

Source: Wendy Bauer, Volunteer Coordinator, San Diego Asian American Repertory Theatre, San Diego, CA. Phone (888) 568-2278. E-mail: volunteers@asianamericanrep.org

---

Bring Out the Leader in Your Volunteers

Is there a volunteer who has been with your organization for some time who you feel may be a great leader? If so, you may want to consider moving them up to the next level in your organization. Whether it's a paid position or a volunteer leadership role, try these tips to get your volunteers to embrace a leadership role:

- Have the volunteer write down their goals by identifying what's important to them.
- Evaluate their strengths and limitations. If a limitation can be improved with training or coursework, identify ways to strengthen that limitation.
- Praise the high level of energy they bring to your volunteer efforts.
- Partner the volunteer with a mentor within your organization to discuss their goals.

NURTURING LEADERS

Advice to Bring Out the Best in Your Volunteers

Training exemplary volunteers to become solid leaders within your volunteer organization not only builds the character of the volunteer, but strengthens your organization as a whole.

Lori Jean Mantooth, director of training and consulting projects, HandsOn Network (Atlanta, GA), offers the following guidance for nurturing volunteer leaders:

What traits must one possess to move from being a volunteer to one who leads volunteers?

"Volunteer leaders possess the skills necessary to organize a service project and lead volunteers effectively in completing that service project. The skill set required for successful volunteer leadership are very similar to the skills required for success in business. Volunteer leadership offers an opportunity to improve upon existing skills and to develop new skills that are broadly applicable."

Some important volunteer leadership skills include:

- Organization
- Communication
- Precision
- Resourcefulness
- Cultural competency
- Delegating
- Problem solving

In what ways can a volunteer exhibit leadership?

"A volunteer leader is a volunteer who leads others in service. Volunteer leaders may plan and/or lead projects; lead others in ongoing service; organize, lead and inspire other volunteers; or represent an organization to volunteers and the community."

Why does having volunteer leaders benefit an organization over handling leadership with staff?

"The community is full of potential leaders, and by tapping into their skills, ideas and passion, an organization can greatly expand the work it does in the community. Volunteer leadership also creates a community of committed leaders who care about and understand the organization's work. Organizations can also increase volunteer retention by offering current volunteers greater responsibility and different opportunities."

What steps are required to nurture a volunteer leader?

"Nurturing volunteer leaders begins with engaging them in meaningful positions. Get to know the volunteer leaders, why they are serving, the skills they have and the ones they want or need to develop. Keep them motivated and engaged through regular training, meetings or even e-mail. Coach and mentor the leaders and support them as they plan projects and lead others. Organizations can pair volunteer leaders to learn from and support each other."

What have your programs done to nurture these volunteer leaders? What steps can nonprofits take to develop volunteer leaders within their organization?

"HandsOn Action Centers use many different methods of nurturing volunteer leaders. In addition to the things noted above, they provide training opportunities, host informal social gatherings at local cafes, and provide support to volunteer leaders as they plan and implement projects. Nonprofits can develop volunteer leaders within their own organizations by identifying leadership roles that volunteers can fill and by recruiting leaders from the current volunteers. They may also choose to approach individual volunteers that possess certain skills or show the potential to develop them. Staff and the potential leader should openly discuss the role, the responsibilities, and what the volunteer leader can expect from stepping into the new role. Promoting volunteers into leadership roles is a great way to recognize volunteers for their service and also increase retention."

How should volunteer leaders be recognized within an organization?

"Recognition is a key component of managing volunteer leaders. It makes the volunteer leaders feel valued and appreciated, increases retention, positions volunteer leaders as people of "authority," builds their credibility with other volunteers and helps recruit additional volunteer leaders. Organizations should examine how they currently recognize volunteers and then determine if or how they should recognize leaders differently. Organizations might consider national volunteer recognition such as the President's Volunteer Service Award, the Daily Point of Light or L'Oreal Women of Worth."

Source: Lori Jean Mantooth, Director of Training and Consulting Projects, HandsOn Network, Atlanta, GA. Phone (404) 979-2900. E-mail: LMantooth@handsonnetwork.org

CONTINUING EDUCATION FOR VOLUNTEERS

How can you go about incorporating continuing education into your volunteer programming? Are there particular topics — such as cross training — that should be a part of your continuing education offerings? What continuing education techniques might you use?

Get Fresh Ideas for In-service Training Topics

Coming up with new and different topics for your continuing education events each year can be challenging. Here's how one volunteer manager keeps trainings fresh.

After 10 years in volunteer management, Jennifer Thompson, coordinator, volunteer and family services, Good Shepherd Hospice (Tulsa, OK), says she was running low on ideas for in-service training programs. So she turned to her volunteers for help.

"Not only do I get new ideas, but when they come up with their own ideas, it gives them ownership of the volunteer program and they're more likely to stay on," Thompson says.

The volunteer coordinator sets the year's first in-service training as a mandatory annual meeting. All of the hospice's volunteers — numbering two dozen — attend, eagerly brainstorming ideas for the six to eight in-service trainings they'll have that year.

Thompson says she leads and guides them, but the volunteers themselves come up with topics they would like to see covered. Some of the volunteer-chosen in-service topics include pet therapy and learning the "friends" approach when dealing with Alzheimer's patients.

An added benefit of involving volunteers is that the volunteers can help reduce presentation costs by making presentations themselves.

Thompson says other volunteers will tape television programs that deal with hospice issues and the volunteers will all watch the programs together for a film night.

Source: Jennifer Thompson, Coordinator of Volunteer and Family Services, Good Shepherd Hospice — Tulsa, Tulsa, OK. Phone (918) 743-5067.
E-mail: Jennifer.Thompson@goodshepherdhospices.com

Couple Recognition With Continuing Education

Scheduling required training at a time that suits all of your volunteers can be tricky. So instead of holding several poorly attended sessions, use highly attended events such as volunteer recognition luncheons to your advantage.

Carla Hummel, director of volunteer services, Avera Sacred Heart (Yankton, SD), first coupled continuing education training with the annual volunteer recognition luncheon three years ago. She has 500 volunteers, a third of whom work in direct patient care and who must pass annual refresher training courses.

Before linking the training and recognition events, Hummel says, she had about 10 percent of volunteers attend the required sessions. This year, by combining the training and luncheon, 60 to 75 percent of those required to undergo the refresher training attended.

To address required training at the volunteer luncheon, Hummel offers a competency fair similar to an open house or job fair. Each topic (privacy and confidentiality, infection control, disaster planning, emergency phone usage, etc.) has its own table staffed by a hospital expert on the subject. Tables are set up in the banquet hall where lunch is served.

Upon arrival, volunteers receive a checklist of topics in which they are required to update their knowledge (see illustration at right). They go from table to table in groups of 10 to 15 to receive training on each topic. Instructors sign off on volunteers' checklists to show they've completed the training. Volunteers place completed checklists in a basket and

Hummel uses them to document training and draw for prizes.

For volunteers who require training but can't attend the event, Hummel writes a quiz from the checklists. She mails or e-mails the quizzes to volunteers, who must pass to continue direct patient care volunteering.

Source: Carla Hummel, Director of Volunteer Services, Avera Sacred Heart, Yankton, SD. Phone (605) 668-8104.
E-mail: chummel@shhservices.com

Content not available in this edition

CONTINUING EDUCATION FOR VOLUNTEERS

Multiple Education Events Benefit Volunteers

Education events are a smart way to keep volunteers motivated. They offer on-going training possibilities, let volunteers see what other positions offer and/or help them deal with stress. According to Treasure Omdahl, coordinator of volunteer services, and Joan Dever, volunteer coordinator, Providence Hospice and Home Care (Everett, WA), the key is to offer frequent events with a lot of choices.

During any month, volunteers can attend at least four education events. They also are invited to staff in-service education events, giving volunteers many options. Omdahl says this is important when it comes to encouraging volunteers to attend events. While the education events aren't mandatory, Omdahl says volunteers are expected to attend at least one annually. She says by keeping the times varied, she can appeal to all volunteers' schedules, giving them more options.

Dever says another encouragement to attend the events is the camaraderie they offer. She says many volunteers work alone, especially in patient care services. The education events give them a chance to socialize with other volunteers.

And, Dever says, socialization time is always something they factor in when planning events.

Omdahl and Dever say putting the education events together is quick and easy. They always have topics in mind, many coming from current events, or they ask the volunteers what topics they'd like addressed. They use available space in-house and ask local experts to come and talk on the topic, making the events practically free to put together.

For example, speakers from Senior Services gave volunteers a presentation on "Depression Screening for the Elderly and Services for the Blind." The presentation was a show-and-tell about things that can help the visually impaired see better. The speakers were happy to educate the volunteers on this topic.

Source: Treasure Omdahl, Coordinator, Volunteer Services, Joan Dever, Volunteer Coordinator, Providence Hospice and Home Care, Everett, WA. Phone (425) 261-4808.
E-mail: treasure.omdahl@providence.org

Make Reading Manuals a Competition

Here's one example of how competition among volunteers can get results, while making it fun for them.

Every crisis counselor at Life Choices Medical Clinic and Resource Center (Joplin, MO), must read the policy and procedure manual every year. As Rita Lawson, client services, says, polices are updated and changed and volunteers need to know them to do their job effectively.

So Lawson divides her 25 to 30 volunteers into teams of three to four people. Each volunteer must initial and date the last page of the manual after they've read it. The team who finishes its manuals first wins dinner out with Lawson.

Lawson says the competition is fierce to get that prize. She says each team pushes the members to read the manuals. She's even had volunteers call her at 10:30 at night to tell her they've finished the manual.

Honesty is not a problem. Lawson says her volunteers are full of integrity and since they have to know what's in the manual, she knows if they haven't read it.

Source: Rita Lawson, Client Services, Life Choices Medical Clinic and Resource Center, Joplin, MO. Phone (417) 623-0131.
E-mail: rital@lifechoices4states.org

Use Different Approaches for Educating Your Volunteers

Even if you provide specialized training for particular volunteer jobs, the process of educating volunteers should be ongoing. Whether your goal is to cross-train volunteers for different jobs, help them to better understand confidentiality issues or to increase their knowledge of your organization's services, education should be ongoing.

To make learning more palatable, use a variety of teaching methods, such as:

- **Case studies.** Share a real-life example with the group and then encourage participants to discuss solutions.

- **Brown bag lunch sessions.** Provide free lunch as an incentive to have a more casual session in which participants discuss a particular topic with the aid of a moderator.

- **Panel of experts.** There may be times when your volunteers would benefit by having experts come in to share their opinions or know how.

- **Values clarification exercise.** Through the use of an experienced facilitator, have the group explore their beliefs about a particular topic in an effort to arrive at some level of consensus.

- **Videotapes/PowerPoint presentations.** This more professional-appearing approach can also be a more entertaining way of holding a group's attention as you educate.

- **Role playing or practice sessions.** There is no better way to learn to do something than through practice. Pair up volunteers and have them work with one another.

CONTINUING EDUCATION FOR VOLUNTEERS

Are You Cross-training Your Volunteers?

Although the value of cross-training volunteers to understand other volunteers' jobs may not be appropriate for every organization, the concept does have its benefits:

1. If others know certain procedures, they can assist when the work load is particularly heavy or regular volunteer workers are absent.

2. Cross-training gives volunteers an appreciation for others' jobs and the contributions each volunteer is making.

3. The notion of all volunteers being trained on others' jobs helps to promote a greater spirit of teamwork and cooperation among everyone.

4. Changing jobs now and then adds variety to volunteers' daily or weekly routines.

5. Bringing in new volunteers from time to time might add an element of competition that will keep "veterans" on their toes.

Build in Yearlong Training

Rather than haphazardly providing volunteer training throughout the year, why not establish a yearlong plan with scheduled workshops?

Identify 12 key topics from which all volunteers can benefit and schedule one workshop each month. You may even choose to repeat more important topics.

Scheduling a series of training opportunities helps would-be participants plan to attend and also helps staff better prepare for each training session.

Knowing training opportunities a year in advance also helps to market them more effectively.

Role-playing Offers Continuing Education for Volunteers

When the Volunteer Center of Southern Arizona (Tuscon, AZ) wants to offer continuing education to its volunteers, they create role-playing opportunities that allow volunteers and staffers a hands-on approach to training.

Amy Knight, Americorps VISTA disaster preparedness coordinator, recently brought together 20 staffers and 35 role-playing volunteers to execute a simulated disaster scenario. The simulation was designed to test the agency's emergency system and procedures in place for staffers and long-term volunteers.

The exercise simulated the evacuation of a senior home, the creation and staffing of a temporary shelter and the use of a volunteer reception center to screen and place spontaneous volunteers to assist at the shelter. In the end, staff of the Volunteer Center of Southern Arizona were able to identify areas in need of improvement should a real disaster strike including necessary revisions to the forms used in the volunteer reception center for clarity and the need for more crowd control staff.

"We've trained volunteers in a classroom for emergency situations, but until we throw them into a realistic situation, it's impossible to know where the weaknesses are," says Knight. "We have to evaluate our systems and volunteers have to practice their skills."

Here are some tips for offering continuing education opportunities for your volunteers through role-playing scenarios:

- Create a simulation scenario to include identities for those role playing. During the simulation at the Volunteer Center of Southern Arizona, identities of potential disaster victims were spelled out on slips of paper and given to staff and volunteers. Those role playing then used that assumed identity to create a "real" scenario.

- Create role-playing identities that specifically challenge the systems you wish to test. If everything goes smoothly and volunteers are only asked to do what they are specifically trained to do, you won't learn as much.

- When creating a role-playing training opportunity, solicit feedback from volunteers and staff to brainstorm a disaster scenario that will test all aspects of your organization.

- Have non-participating staff members evaluate the role-playing event to be witness to the process and to identify ways in which things can be improved for a real crisis.

- Conduct a debriefing of those involved in the role-playing event. Evaluate the process and determine what was learned and put in place the steps to correct any areas that were weak during the simulation.

Source: Amy Knight, Americorps VISTA Disaster Preparedness Coordinator, Volunteer Center of Southern Arizona, Tucson, AZ. Phone (520) 881-3300. E-mail: aknight@volunteersoaz.org

CONTINUING EDUCATION FOR VOLUNTEERS

Offer Volunteers Flexible Continuing Ed Options

Volunteers at Jackson County Court Appointed Special Advocates (CASA) of Kansas City, MO are required to complete 12 hours of continuing education each year. To make it easier for them to meet this requirement, the nonprofit offers flexible training options.

"We offer in-house, in-service training throughout the year, but we also allow our volunteers to use college courses, classes offered in the community or other organizations' in-service trainings to count for their yearly hours," explains Karrie Krumm, senior case supervisor/volunteer management.

Of these, Krumm says the monthly in-services offered by Jackson County CASA are the most popular option with 10 to 15 of the organization's volunteers typically attending each training.

When offering this type of continuing education opportunity, Krumm offers the following advice:

- **Give plenty of notice and send reminders.**
- **Follow up.** "See what they found to be useful or not," Krumm says. "Listen to what your volunteers are telling you they want to learn about. They are a great source of ideas."
- **Make sessions volunteer-friendly.** "We do a lot of lunch and learns or early evening trainings," she says. "Offering light snacks and an opportunity for networking are big draws."
- **Invite staff.** Krumm says her volunteers enjoy the opportunity to visit with staff, which helps the volunteers feel connected to the organization.

Although the organization's own in-services are the most popular option, Krumm recognizes the value in accepting other trainings for continuing education credit.

"We chose to let them use other methods

of continuing ed because we realize how difficult it may be to utilize our trainings for all 12 hours they are supposed to do each year," she says. "There is also a lot of good information out there, and it just makes sense to let them use those hours. We appreciate the time they spend on their volunteer work, and we want to make it as easy as possible for them to achieve their hours."

Additionally, she says, "The advantage to this method is that more volunteers are going to do their in-service hours, and gain a lot of knowledge in the process," she says. "This makes for a better advocate for the kids we represent. It also helps them stay involved and bring information to the table that we may not have had otherwise."

Even though Jackson County CASA volunteers may turn to other organizations for training opportunities, they must submit paperwork to obtain credit. For instance, volunteers attending workshops not offered by Jackson County CASA are required to write a one-page summary to address areas such as:

- What were the issues discussed?
- What were the strengths and weaknesses of the workshop?
- What were the outcomes?
- What were your overall thoughts or opinions of the workshop?

Those opting to take a college course that addresses relevant topics like child development, family law, child abuse and neglect, or communications with children, need to submit his or her final grade card with a copy of the course description.

Source: Karrie Krumm, Senior Case Supervisor/ Volunteer Management, Jackson County CASA, Kansas City, MO. Phone (816) 842-2272, ext. 204. E-mail: karrie@jacksoncountycasa-mo.org

Volunteer Training Primer: Principles, Procedures and Ideas for Training and Educating Volunteers.
Edited by Scott C. Stevenson.
© 2009 Stevenson, Inc. Published 2009 by Stevenson, Inc.

SPECIALIZED TRAINING & EDUCATION

Many volunteer positions require specialized training. This chapter is intended to address some of those more specialized positions (e.g., docents, chaplains, teens, episodic volunteers, interpreters and more).

Training Intense for Potential Docents

Most volunteers are required to participate in some type of training. However, the intensity of the training significantly increases when that volunteer is a docent.

Here, two professionals — Nanette Simonds, director of education and library services, Rocky Mountain Quilt Museum (Golden, CO), and Rachel Arbogast, docent coordinator, St. Louis Zoo Education Department, Docent Organization (St. Louis, MO) — share their training procedures and advice for others with docent programs.

Organization: Rocky Mountain Quilt Museum (Golden, CO)

Number of Docents: 40

Initial Training: "Our docent training consists of five weeks of 2.5 hours per week," explains Nanette Simonds, director of education and library services. She says topics include:

- History of American quilting
- Tour techniques
- Storytelling for the docent
- Quilt color, pattern and design
- Educational level
- Three elements of a good tour
- Greeter/docent duties

Simonds says the museum may soon invite experts from special areas of interest, such as quilt historians and folklorists, to do portions of the training.

In addition to the classes, Simonds says, "Homework is required, such as research of a particular topic in quilting and required visits to other museums to study other gallery situations and touring techniques. This information is then discussed with the group in training."

Continuing Education: "We continually update the information about general topics, as well as specific and special exhibits and events," Simonds explains.

Advice: "Know both your museum's mission and your volunteers as a resource," she says. "Offer relevant training beyond the basics. Make the volunteer experience a joyful and growing experience."

Organization: St. Louis Zoo (St. Louis, MO)

Number of Docents: 250

Initial Training: Volunteers attend a two-day training. First day is volunteer orientation. Second day focuses on zoo information. "Those are prerequisites for the docent program," says Rachel Arbogast, docent coordinator. Offered at least once a year, docent training consists of a weekly class for 13 weeks. Between classes docents have homework and appointments with a mentor, an active docent. Docents receive training in all areas of the zoo.

Main training topics include:

- interpretation techniques,
- principles of interpretation and education,
- basic biology concepts,
- zoology of each animal area, and
- conservation, both zoo and personal.

Continuing Education: To keep docents up to date, the zoo offers annual training in areas such as tours and outreach training. Additionally, there are continuing education events held twice a month.

Advice: "Have guest speakers and subject area experts as often as possible," Arbogast says. "Those are really the best and most memorable for them. Also, any time you can involve them or give them an experience the general public does not get to do makes them feel special and it helps to motivate them in training and keep them interested in the program."

*Sources: Nanette Simonds, Director of Education and Library Services, Rocky Mountain Quilt Museum, Golden, CO.
Phone (303) 277-0377. E-mail: nanette_s@rmqm.org. Website: www.rmqm.org
Rachel Arbogast, Docent Coordinator, St. Louis Zoo Education Department, Docent Organization, St. Louis, MO.
Phone (314) 781-0900. E-mail: arbogast@stlzoo.org. Website: www.stlzoo.org*

SPECIALIZED TRAINING & EDUCATION

How to Recruit and Prepare Volunteer Chaplains

Volunteer chaplains play an important role in numerous nonprofit organizations. Al Henager, staff chaplain and coordinator of palliative care, University of Arkansas for Medical Services (Little Rock, AR), says, "The key to an effective volunteer chaplain program is that the program be supervised by a clinically trained chaplain who is also certified by one of the nationally recognized chaplain credentialing bodies. This gives integrity and credibility to the program and assures quality."

Once this has been established, the nonprofit can focus on recruiting and training the best individuals to serve its organization.

What are the best recruitment and training methods to build an effective volunteer chaplain program? Henager says these three methods should be combined to successfully recruit volunteer chaplains:

1. **Personal recruiting.** "This is the single most effective method I have found for recruiting, because it involves building relationships with people," says Henager. He makes connections with fellow pastors, ministers and other clergy through professional organizations such as the ministerial alliance and by visiting congregations, speaking to Sunday School classes, ladies' auxiliaries, men's groups, study groups, etc.

2. **Mass recruiting.** Tactics such as mass mailing letters, recruitment dinners and recruitment educational events are also an effective recruitment tool.

3. **Word-of-mouth recruiting.** "Gradually, as people become more involved, they start inviting their friends and colleagues, and recruitment comes by way of word of mouth," says Henager.

Once a chaplain is chosen, the next step is to offer appropriate training. While most nonprofit volunteer departments have volunteer policies and procedures in place, volunteer chaplains should receive training beyond the organization's required training modules.

Volunteer chaplains under Henager's supervision receive a facility tour and training in:

- Program overview and commitment
- Institutional orientation and health screenings
- Introduction to pastoral care and pastoral identity
- Establishing the helping relationship
- Effective active listening skills
- Creating understanding
- Ministering in crisis and grief situations
- Ministering to the confused and disoriented
- Ministering to the elderly
- Understanding and using pastoral assessment

- Suicide prevention
- Ministering to children in death and dying
- Overview and practice in implementing policies and procedures

Pastoral volunteers also require policy training, including:

- Policies on program vision
- Policy on scope and plan of care
- Organization policy
- Requirements and expectations policy
- Policy on proselytizing
- Procedures on daily visits/rounds
- Procedures on response to emergencies (e.g., codes, death, etc.)
- Policy and procedure on documentation
- Policy and procedure for confidentiality/HIPAA
- Policy and procedure for response to disasters

Source: Al Henager, Staff Chaplain and Coordinator of Palliative Care, University of Arkansas for Medical Sciences, Little Rock, AR. Phone (501) 686-5410. E-mail: aahenager@uams.edu

---

Types of Volunteer Chaplains

Al Henager, staff chaplain and coordinator of palliative care, University of Arkansas for Medical Services (Little Rock, AR), oversees clergy volunteers and lay volunteers.

Henager explains the differences between the types of pastoral caregivers:

- **Clergy volunteers** are ordained ministers in good standing with their faith group; have college, seminary and clinical pastoral education; and/or meet their own faith group's educational requirements. The person must have the blessing and approval of their faith group or congregation to serve as a volunteer. In a hospital, clergy volunteers are generalists in pastoral care, making rounds every day and are on-call at night for crises such as codes, deaths and other emergencies. They also make referrals to the staff chaplain and are first-line visitors for newly admitted and pre-surgery patients.

- **Lay volunteers** are persons affiliated with a recognized congregational/faith group but do not serve as an ordained minister. These persons must have three solid references and be endorsed or commissioned by their faith group or congregation. These volunteers serve as eucharistic ministers, office/clerical helpers and pastoral visitors who make hospitality visits to new patients, distribute approved literature, do basic initial pastoral screenings and visit with family and friends in the waiting rooms.

SPECIALIZED TRAINING & EDUCATION

On-call Volunteers Keep Center Available 24 Hours a Day

While the Family Sunshine Center (Montgomery, AL) is a fully staffed domestic violence crisis center during the weekdays, 26 on-call hotline volunteers staff the 24-hour crisis line in the evenings and weekends.

Sally Beane, volunteer coordinator, explains the important role on-call hotline volunteers play in the center's daily operations:

What are the on-call hotline volunteers' job duties?

"Volunteers are asked to work at least two crisis line shifts per month from their homes, (5 p.m. to midnight during the week, and 8 a.m. to 4 p.m. or 4 p.m. to midnight on the weekend). They provide support and information to domestic violence victims; help identify the caller's needs; ask screening questions to determine if the caller meets the center's shelter criteria; educate victims about our resources; and maintain phone call documentation and records of all information relayed to the caller. If approved for shelter, we will meet the victim at a designated safe place to transport them to our facility. If our services aren't what they're looking for, our volunteers refer them to a more applicable community resource."

What qualifications must a hotline volunteer possess?

"I'm looking for people who are non-judgmental and empathetic, who understand the dynamics of domestic violence and are willing to provide the victim/caller with information and options to make their own decision. They should be familiar with our mission and services, as well as other community resources, possess the ability to work cooperatively with staff and possess auto insurance so they can transport a victim to a safe place if the need arises."

What training must a hotline volunteer receive?

"Our volunteers receive extensive training. Our training is typically four to five 2.5 to 3-hour sessions held in a two-week timeframe, plus four hours of observation with a shelter night manager. Even after the training and observation period, if we or the volunteer feels they may need additional time before being placed on the schedule, we will place them with the house manager for further observation until we feel they meet our standards and they feel they are ready."

Why is it important to know you have the right hotline volunteers?

"Many times the crisis line is the first point of contact for a person caught in a domestic violence situation, and we must have the right people in those roles. If a volunteer does not have the right attitude, knowledge about the dynamics of domestic violence and familiarity with our resources, the caller will not get what they need, and they may not call back. This could be the only time they seek help, and it's crucial that volunteers are well-trained, have the ability to empathize and offer options to help victims do what is in their best interest."

Source: Sally Beane, Volunteer Coordinator, Family Sunshine Center, Montgomery, AL. Phone (334) 206-2120. E-mail: sbeane@familysunshine.org

Content not available in this edition

SPECIALIZED TRAINING & EDUCATION

Tips for Training Tour Guides

- Ask visitors to complete a brief tour evaluation. An occasional evaluation distributed to visitors following a guided tour will provide candid feedback on ways your tour guides can improve. Allow anonymity and offer a small token of appreciation for having taken the time to complete the evaluation.

- After your guides have mastered tour basics, spoon-feed them additional information that they can be prepared to share as further points of interest to visitors.

- Conduct practice tours using employees and videotape each volunteer tour guide so he/she can view him/herself in action.

Train Teens for Challenging Assignments

When Barbara Mross came on the job five years ago as director of volunteer services with Bayhealth Medical Center (Milford, DE), she immediately recognized a problem: Nurses in the hospital's medical-surgical units were too busy to train teen volunteers and didn't know how to put the volunteers to use in the busy department.

So Mross quickly turned that problem into an opportunity to both enhance her volunteers' training and nurture a better relationship between volunteers and hospital staff.

Mross met with the hospital's education department to develop a "Teen Volunteer Patient Care Orientation" training class. Offered after a general orientation, the class teaches hand-on training to teens who want to work with patient care.

Taught by the hospital's clinical educator, the classes give teens an opportunity to get to know each other as they develop important skills through hands-on training that includes wheelchair transport, confidentiality issues and more.

Thanks to the training, Mross says, the teens come to the medical-surgical units confident and ready to volunteer in an area they might have otherwise had reservations about approaching. Plus, they have had an opportunity to meet some hospital staff, and staff, in turn, have gotten to know them through the training.

"We tell them, 'Your volunteer experience is what you make it,' now they are more comfortable with what they are doing there," she says.

Mross says the class has helped the teen volunteers make huge steps forward with the staff. The staff now appreciates knowing the teens are coming to their units already trained and ready to work.

To help reassure staff who may still be reluctant about working with the young volunteers, Mross provides them with a list of guidelines that she requires the teens to follow. The teens, she says, are trained to do everything an adult volunteer does, except transport specimens.

Source: Barbara Mross, Volunteer Services Director, Bayhealth Medical Center/Milford Memorial Hospital, Milford, DE. Phone (302) 430-5621. E-mail: Barbara_mross@bayhealth.org

Hands-on Training Prepares Teens to Volunteer

At Bayhealth Medical Center (Milford, DE), teens who volunteer on the medical-surgical floor go through a "Teen Volunteer Care Orientation" developed by Barbara Mross, director of volunteer services.

The training, Mross says, is all about hands-on learning to make the class fun and educational for the youth volunteers while also preparing them for the challenging assignment.

Among the topics covered in the orientation are:

✓ **Confidentiality** — First, HIPPA and the hospital's own confidentiality requirements are reiterated.

✓ **Meal service** — Using an actual food service tray, the teens are trained how to recognize what's on a tray, how to remove lids, clear the area for the tray, help fill out menus and assist patients with their meals without feeding them.

✓ **Identification** — Teens take turns learning to read actual hospital arm bands and a patient's room board.

✓ **Wheelchair transport** — The volunteers take turns practicing on getting each other in and out of wheelchairs, how to enter and exit an elevator with a wheelchair and how to keep the patient safe inside the chair.

✓ **Bed making** — Using an actual hospital bed, teens learn the proper bed-making techniques with a teen on each side.

✓ **General information** — The teens get the low down on operating and adjusting everything in a patient's room, from running the TV, to lights, to call bells, how to handle complaints and concerns, and how to talk with the patient.

SPECIALIZED TRAINING & EDUCATION

Consider Family Volunteer Opportunities

Volunteering as a family is one way for volunteers to fulfill their giving commitments while teaching children giving values. Heather Jack, president, The Volunteer Family (Framingham, MA), has worked for more than five years matching family volunteers with worthy causes through The Volunteer Family website at www.thefamilyvolunteer.org. Nearly 30,000 family volunteer opportunities are listed at the site to assist families in finding ways in which they can volunteer as a unit.

Are family volunteers a good fit for nonprofits? A recent Bridgespan survey found that 98 percent of social service agencies using family volunteers found them to be very effective volunteers.

"Family volunteering helps nonprofit organizations broaden their services and their community outreach while improving public image and relations," says Jack.

One significant benefit for working with family volunteers is that bringing families on board to fill volunteer needs offers nonprofits the opportunity to bring young volunteers into the organization who offer energy, enthusiasm and a volunteer base for future, long-term volunteers.

A 2005 Corporation for National and Community Service study showed that youth from a family where at least one parent volunteered were two times more likely to volunteer as adults.

"Working with volunteering families is a natural multiplier of volunteers for any nonprofit organization," Jack says. "And, by working with youth, you are setting the basis for some potentially lifelong volunteers."

Training family volunteers requires a unique approach. Here are some important training tips for creating a beneficial family volunteer arrangement:

- Determine whether the family can participate in your organization's standard training schedule. If not, create training times that accommodate a family schedule.

- Consider creating a modified training session that accommodates families and the attention spans of younger volunteers. Conduct one-on-one training sessions per family as an ideal way to engage all family members during the training process.

- Create a handout or training manual that is brief and pointed, allowing families to review the information more thoroughly at home.

- Offer a family volunteer job description for their role within the organization and offer orientation geared specifically for this unique brand of volunteer group.

- Assign the parents or guardians the role of "leader" so that they take on the task of organizing their family unit as a volunteer entity. Assign one point person for all direct communication from the nonprofit.

- Recognize each individual in the family volunteer unit. Assign roles to each person within the family, outlining the specific roles and tasks they should complete. Clearly defined roles for each member allows the family to function better as a group.

- Don't forget about the smaller members of the family volunteer unit. Even small children can contribute to the effort, but they may need to be assigned a less intensive role or task.

- During the orientation, communicate to all members of the family unit and not only the adults. Be sure to communicate the purpose and the mission of the organization to youth as well as adults.

- Evaluate the organization's environment. Provide a safe, comfortable training and working environment conducive to family volunteer units.

- Find ways to recognize each individual for their contributions as well as thanking the family as a unit.

Source: Heather Jack, President, The Volunteer Family, Framingham, MA. Phone (508) 861-0560. E-mail: hjack@thevolunteerfamily.org

---

How to Find Family Volunteers

Could your organization benefit from the help of family volunteers but you are unsure where to find them?

Here are a few ways to locate potential family volunteers:

- Distribute flyers at a local community event.
- Blog about your opportunities at local family-oriented websites.
- Be sure to mention opportunities at your organization's functions.

SPECIALIZED TRAINING & EDUCATION

Train Volunteers to Lead Education Programs

Community education events are an essential part of promoting your organization's mission. According to Heather House, supervisor of volunteer services and programs, Toronto Zoo (Toronto, Ontario, Canada), allowing volunteers to provide educational presentations makes sense because with volunteer help, more programs can get delivered to the community.

The Toronto Zoo has outreach education volunteers who give presentations to groups on 13 curriculum-related topics and operate touch tables (theme-based tables with accompanying facts) at community and zoo events. These volunteers need enough training to be knowledgeable about their subject and to present the right image for the zoo.

Volunteers go through a 13-week training course, which includes these components:

- Presentations and/or tours with curators from zoo departments (e.g., mammals, fish, horticulture, reptiles, birds and invertebrates).

- Appropriate messages to give, dos and don'ts and how to handle certain questions from the marketing and public relations departments and zoo education segments.

- Engaging and interpreting visitors and touch table tactics.

- How and where to use information about formal and informal zoo education programs.

- Zoo operation, emergency procedures and security protocols.

- A wrap-up session to review zoo policies and procedures on speaking with the public.

- Specialized sessions on PowerPoint presentations, what a good presentation entails and presentation scripts.

Based on comfort level, volunteers can shadow an experienced outreach volunteer before going out on their own. Follow-up training is given for script changes and updated information on zoo departments and programs.

Source: Heather House, Supervisor of Volunteer Services and Programs, Toronto Zoo, Toronto, Ontario, Canada. Phone (416) 392-5943. E-mail: hhouse@torontozoo.ca

vMentors — A Program Making a Big Difference

These days many nonprofit organizations use virtual volunteers — persons who work from a computer either on site or from home to fulfill a volunteer role.

One such nonprofit is the Orphan Foundation of America (OFA) of Sterling, VA.

OFA staffs 300 virtual volunteers to mentor teens with its vMentor program. This "cognitive coaching" matches teens in the OFA program with mentors who are interested in their success and guidance for their futures.

Founded in 1981, OFA serves thousands of foster teens across the United States. With the help of vMentors, 366 of those teens are given guidance by adult vMentor volunteers by way of e-mail dialogue, guiding the teens to make good decisions.

"We don't want the mentors to answer their questions, we want the mentors to guide the mentees to creating their own answers," says Lynn Davis, manager of partnership development.

How can your organization best utilize virtual volunteers?

- **Offer a structured training program** — Volunteers working within the vMentor program must complete an extensive virtual training program and participate in monthly trainings to volunteer as mentors to OFA teens. Mentors are trained to guide students to draw their own conclusions instead of offering them a direct answer to the problem.

- **Monitor all communications** — In OFA's case, all communications are done on secure portals and are monitored by staff to ensure the safety of the mentored teens.

- **Offer ongoing training and consistent contact with virtual volunteers** — vMentor volunteers participate in monthly trainings and support sessions headed by OFA staff to keep the program on track.

Participation in the vMentor program is a decision made by the teen. Teens mentored within the vMentor program are twice as likely to graduate than those who do not accept mentoring, says Davis, noting: "vMentors help our kids stay motivated to stay in college."

Lynn Davis, Manager of Partnership Development, Orphan Foundation of America, Sterling, VA. Phone (571) 203-0270. E-mail: ldavis@orphan.org. Website: www.orphan.org

SPECIALIZED TRAINING & EDUCATION

Eliminate Future Confusion: Give Mentors a Checklist During Training

Mentors require extensive training to be able to handle the numerous situations that can arise working with volunteers and clients.

Debra Tucker, volunteer coordinator, Pregnancy Care Center (Springfield, MO), found many of her organization's mentors had numerous questions about their duties even after being trained. To help eliminate some of those questions and allow both volunteers and staff to feel more comfortable with the training, she created a three-page "Mentor Checklist."

Volunteers, staff and Tucker all gave input as to what to include.

Shown in part at right, the checklist includes items volunteer mentors need to complete before starting on their own. The checklist is given to the volunteers once they arrive for training. Tasks can be completed at the volunteer's own pace, but Tucker says staff encourages them to complete training and start volunteering as soon as they are able.

Once they complete the checklist, it is reviewed by a staff supervisor.

Tucker says that besides offering a more complete training procedure, the checklist allows trainees to feel confident that when they have completed the list of requirements, they are better qualified to handle the position.

The checklist is done in addition to shadow training with other mentors.

The organization's mentors serve as confidantes to pregnant women and provide support and resources to expectant mothers, fathers and parents.

Source: Debra Tucker, Volunteer Coordinator, Pregnancy Care Center, Springfield, MO. Phone (417) 877-0800. E-mail: volunteers@pcchoices.org

Content not available in this edition

A comprehensive mentor checklist, shown in part here, helps guarantee volunteers with the Pregnancy Care Center (Springfield, MO) are trained for and understand their duties.

SPECIALIZED TRAINING & EDUCATION

Offer Training for High Stress Positions

"Taking Care of Ourselves" is the motto and the title of a special training session for volunteers at the Women's Resource Center of the NRV (Radford, VA).

Volunteers at the Women's Resource Center work directly with victims of domestic violence and sexual assault, putting them at high risk for burnout and compassion fatigue.

Over the years, two seasoned volunteers, Eliott Chamberlin-Long and Kathryn Ryder, used their experience and developed materials and content for combating stress. "'Taking Care of Ourselves' touches on: healthy habits, stress relievers and emotional health. "We asked participants to reflect on quotes about boundaries and list examples of how stress and vicarious traumatization (compassion fatigue) manifest within them and also ways they currently manage it," say Chamberlin-Long and Ryder.

✓ **Healthy habits** — There is information on the handouts about overall health, and preventing stress from taking too great of a toll. Exercise, eating well and getting enough sleep are highlighted.

✓ **Stress relievers** — We provide handouts with lots of ideas, and we demonstrate several different techniques, such as breathing meditation, which can be done anywhere, any time. We also demonstrate progressive muscle relaxation and imagery.

✓ **Emotional health** — During the section on boundaries, the focus is directly on emotional health, learning to say no and developing a safe and healthy 'filter' for things we let in and keep out of our lives. When we talk about secondary traumatization, we point out how hearing others' stories can affect emotional health by changing the way we think about the world. During the brainstorming of stress-reduction ideas, participants often touch on strategies for emotional release in the way of journaling, talking to friends, or taking a break from stressful situations.

"When people deal with crisis on a regular basis, there are bound to be some negative results. This presentation is intended to 'head it off at the pass.' We cannot run our program effectively if we don't allow our volunteers the time and space to take care of themselves and give them permission to work out their issues," says Mary Forti, volunteer coordinator.

Source: Eliott Chamberlin-Long and Kathryn Ryder, Volunteers, Mary Forti, Volunteer Coordinator, Women's Resource Center, Radford, VA. Phone (540) 639-1123. E-mail: volunteers@wrcnrv.org

Stress Relief Through Relaxation

1. **Deep breathing** — Breathe in deeply through the nose, letting your stomach expand as much as possible. Once you have breathed in as much as possible, hold your breath for a few seconds and then exhale slowly through your mouth. Repeat three to four times several times a day.

2. **Active relaxation** — Tense then relax each muscle of the body. Start with the muscles in your head and move down to your feet.

3. **Stretching exercises** — By sitting or standing at your workstation you can stretch your shoulders, arms, back, sides, neck, wrists, hands and forearms. To stretch your hands spread out your fingers until you feel a gentle stretch, relax and close. Repeat 10 to 15 times per hand.

4. **Visualization** — Visualize a successful outcome to a stressful situation. Or visualize a peaceful scene, such as ocean waves lapping on a beach to create relaxation.

5. **Passive relaxation** — Meditate once or twice a day for 10 to 20 minutes in a quiet place while concentrating on a point of focus, having a passive accepting attitude and a comfortable position.

6. **Yoga** — Slow, deliberate postures with carefully controlled breathing.

7. **Biofeedback** — Send direct messages to various parts of the body to get a desired response. For example, people have been able to prevent frostbite by sending a message to their hands to stay warm. Also used to control chronic pain.

What Volunteers Said About the Training

Things I liked:

- Demonstration of relaxation techniques
- Exercises
- Great interactions and demonstration
- Breathing exercises
- I really liked the responsible to/ responsible for distinction. And I always like a chance to breathe.
- The meditation exercise and stress preventing tips
- Relaxation techniques
- I liked that the speakers gave us ideas about how to take care of ourselves emotionally and physically. I think these will be much needed and used.
- Quotes. Breathing.
- Relaxation techniques
- Pie. Quotes.
- Laying on the floor
- Breathing exercise
- Loved the meditation. Liked the stress busters. Elliot/ Kathryn are awesome.
- Learning stress. Relaxation techniques.

SPECIALIZED TRAINING & EDUCATION

Student Volunteers Bring Energy, Enthusiasm

At the Kidzu Children's Museum (Chapel Hill, NC), learning is a hands-on adventure driven by a strong volunteer workforce.

This interactive museum for children and families has hosted a series of nationally recognized exhibits including "Where the Wild Things Are" and "Mister Rogers' Neighborhood." In any given semester, at least 40 volunteers help with programs and assist the museum's 400 members.

Workstudy students from the local college assist in staffing 90 percent of the museum's volunteer positions. Local high school students serve as volunteers to fulfill community service requirements.

These relationships create a win-win situation for the students and the museum, helping to create a volunteer base while providing the young volunteers with an opportunity to build their reference and resume file.

Tina Clossick, director of operations, shares some of the techniques she uses to help prepare the museum's young volunteers for their many tasks:

- **Training is key to the success of the volunteer.** The museum's traveling exhibits require ongoing training so volunteers become knowledgeable about each incoming exhibit. Volunteers receive one-hour trainings to learn the details of each new exhibit.
- **Teach early childhood techniques.** Volunteers learn to identify the ability of the child and help the child stretch his/her knowledge.

- **Model the behavior you would like student volunteers to emulate.** In training, Kidzu volunteers role-play to become efficient at techniques needed to work with young children and parents.

- **Train the volunteers to be supervisors, not disciplinarians.** The volunteer learns to keep the area safe for children and artful distraction techniques if a child misbehaves. Volunteers seek out caregivers for disciplinary needs.

- **Customer service is a critical component.** Like any other service-based organization, Kidzu requires strong customer service orientation from its volunteers. Volunteers are trained to not only answer a question, but to give more than what's asked for by offering more details. For example, they not only point out where the restroom is, but explain that changing tables are available for little ones.

Clossick says she finds working with youth volunteers to be a great advantage as they are easy to work with and have high energy levels. Volunteers age 15 to 22 also tend to have flexible schedules, which is conducive to the museum's operations.

Source: Tina Clossick, Director of Operations, Kidzu Museum, Chapel Hill, NC. Phone (919) 933-1455. E-mail: clossick@mindspring.com

---

Three Steps Improve Student Volunteer Success

The Kidzu Museum (Chapel Hill, NC) welcomes high school and college students for volunteering roles. But working with young people can pose some challenges, says Tina Clossick, director of operations.

Here, she offers three tips for helping young volunteers succeed:

1. If friends want to volunteer together, offer each a separate task to avoid talking and distraction.

2. Volunteers at Kidzu are required to call if they'll be more than 10 minutes late. Consistent tardiness can lead to dismissal, but Clossick assures reminders do the trick.

3. To avoid lackluster performance and keep young volunteers energized, give daily feedback and stress the positive. Offer constructive criticism, but also chat with volunteers one on one about their lives to create a warm, friendly atmosphere.

Nurture Episodic Volunteers Between Projects

Not all of your volunteers show up weekly for regularly scheduled tasks. There are those volunteers whose assistance is limited to the duration of particular projects. Their services are only needed now and then (e.g., during a twice-a-year phonathon, making deliveries on a monthly basis, etc.).

Because of the sporadic contact with your organization, it's possible for this type of volunteer to lose interest in your cause if he/she remains out of touch with what's happening. "Out of sight; out of mind," so to speak. Because of this, it's a good idea to create a system to nurture episodic volunteers during those down times when they're not assisting your agency. To help keep them motivated and ready to pitch in when called on, bolster their enthusiasm by:

✓ Including them among those who receive a monthly one- or two-page "what's happening" agency update.

✓ Allowing them to witness the fruits of their labor by showing them the results of past projects in which they have been involved.

✓ Making sure they are extended the invitation to become involved in additional volunteer projects outside the scope of their past involvement.

✓ Coming up with special recognition measures that show these volunteers your appreciation — a picnic, a local newspaper ad listing their names, a letter of commendation to their employers.

SPECIALIZED TRAINING & EDUCATION

Learn Key Topics Necessary When Training Volunteer Interpreters

Does the community serviced by your organization, support the need for volunteer interpreters? According to Andrea Rander, former director, volunteer services and language interpreters program, National Institutes of Health, Clinic Center (Bethesda, MD), with more than 300 languages spoken in the United States, nonprofits are seeing a growing need for this select group of volunteers.

For this reason it is crucial these volunteers receive the training necessary to give the people they serve a voice.

If your organization requires the need of volunteer interpreters, Rander says training should include:

- Language proficiency,
- Ethics and boundaries,
- Confidentiality,
- Responding to agency staff,
- Recognizing diversity issues,
- Being a cultural broker,
- Representing the agency you interpret for,
- Awareness of the agency's mission, and
- Good communication skills.

Although each is significant, Rander focuses on three topics:

Proficiency

"Volunteer interpreters should be required to be proficient in the language they are to interpret, particularly if they are interpreting in a medical or legal arena," Rander explains. "Any distortion of a word or phrase could be devastating to the case involved. For example, in the medical arena, the word for '11' in Spanish is 'ounce.' If a patient receives a prescription for medication and is asked to take an ounce of the medicine and the interpreter incorrectly interprets the prescription for 11 instead of ounce, the outcome is obvious."

To ensure proficiency, Rander recommends testing for accuracy and fluency, as well as a vital component — good listening skills.

"It is not always easy to sense if the applicant will have decent communication skills when the volunteer has signed up, but testing is one way to begin the process of determining those skills," she says.

Ethics and Boundaries

It is imperative that volunteer interpreters understand and adhere to ethical and confidentiality policies. Both the nonprofit and the client are putting complete trust in the volunteer interpreter. Under no circumstances may he or she reveal information to another party.

Additionally, Rander says volunteer interpreters must

recognize and respect boundaries. Often clients develop a bond with interpreters and will occasionally ask for personal information such as a phone number or for a favor like borrowing money. A trainer must make the volunteer interpreter understand the importance of maintaining a strictly professional relationship with clients.

Cultural Broker

Rander says the role of a volunteer interpreter extends beyond interpretation.

"He or she is a cultural broker who understands the nuances; the fabric of the culture of the client; the influence and possibly the politics of the country from which the client comes," she explains. "In support of the client, the volunteer interpreter must be able to convey to the party in need of the interpreting how to best approach the client in a way not to offend his or her beliefs and ideas."

Training Methods

Now that you understand what to teach volunteer interpreters, Rander offers advice on how to teach this group of volunteers.

- **Provide a verbal orientation accompanied by a written manual.** Be sure to update the manual regularly to include new or revised information.

- **Provide a shadowing experience.** She says pairing a new volunteer with an experienced interpreter is a great training technique.

- **Role-play.** Ask an experienced interpreter to role-play with new volunteers. As the training progresses, have them switch roles to further the learning experience.

- **Show videos** to assist in training volunteer interpreters.

- **Assign a mentor.** By the time the agency assigns the new volunteer his or her first client, most of the formal training will have occurred. However, Rander recommends that a mentor accompany the new interpreter on his or her first assignment. "This observation will enable the mentor to point out any errors in judgment, errors in clarity and in accuracy," she says.

- **Provide ongoing training and support.** These opportunities allow volunteers to address problems, share techniques and offer suggestions.

Source: Andrea Rander, Retired Director of Volunteer Services and Language Interpreters Programs, National Institutes of Health, Clinic Center, Bethesda, MD. Phone (301) 530-9085. E-mail: randrea847@yahoo.com

SPECIALIZED TRAINING & EDUCATION

Prepare Volunteer Training for Those 50-plus

Is there a way to better train those members of your volunteer department who are 50 and over, than your other volunteers?

While it is important to not segregate them from your other volunteers, it is important to recognize that this group of volunteers has characteristics unique to its generation.

Andrea Taylor, director of training, Temple University Center for Intergenerational Learning/College of Health Professions (Philadelphia, PA), says as a volunteer coordinator it is important to be aware of these characteristics so training can be tailored to the specific age group.

Taylor categorizes these volunteers into three groups: GI Generation (born 1912-1927), post war/silent generation (born 1928-1945), and boomers (born 1946-1964).

Individuals in these groups experienced a variety of "defining moments" (e.g., war, major disasters, economic conditions, social issues and technological developments).

"Defining moments influence an age cohort's values and attitudes about life and family, work/retirement and community involvement," says Taylor.

She offers the following suggestions when training individuals 50 or older:

- **Offer an overview.** Cover the scope of the volunteer work (time commitment, skills needed and reporting mechanisms); the organization's and project's mission and goals; and the roles volunteers play in the organization's structure.

- **Be sensitive.** Choose your words wisely, warns Taylor. For instance, when training people in the GI Generation, Taylor suggests using the word "volunteering," while adjusting your terminology to words such as "community work" or "pro-bono consulting" when training boomers. Words suggesting leadership may be useful when training boomers, such as "activists" and "managers,"

while terms such as "senior citizen" can raise a red flag. Instead, Taylor recommends referring to these groups as 50-plus.

- **Choose your training method carefully.** Since many boomers are comfortable with technology, Taylor says consider a PowerPoint presentation to enhance the training experience. Older volunteers, however, prefer a more hands-on approach.

- **Provide visuals.** Visual reinforcements are always beneficial in training. However, make sure handouts are easy to read, using large print and bullet points for easy reference. When possible, use compelling photos.

- **Draw on experience.** Volunteers who are 50 and older have many real-world experiences and want to feel valued for their knowledge. Consider inviting these volunteers to share their experiences throughout your training.

- **Use an emotional appeal.** Back up the facts with a story. "Remember, all the research in the world doesn't grab people the way a story does."

- **Team up with a 50-plus volunteer.** If you are uncomfortable as a volunteer coordinator supervising a volunteer twice your age, Taylor recommends asking an experienced 50-plus volunteer for assistance. They can provide valuable information and may be able to better relate with the volunteers in training.

To learn more about working with volunteers 50 and older, visit http://cil.templecil.org.

Source: Andrea Taylor, Ph.D., Director of Training, Temple University Center for Intergenerational Learning/College of Health Professions, Philadelphia, PA. Phone (215) 204-6970. E-mail: ataylor@temple.edu

SPECIALIZED TRAINING & EDUCATION

Five Topics to Address With Corporate Volunteers

Businesses turn to corporate volunteerism for many reasons — to build employee skills, to increase cooperation or to obtain good publicity. As the nonprofit welcoming these volunteers, it is important to provide quality training to make the experience mutually rewarding.

"Volunteering can offer a very rewarding experience to employees and just takes some basic planning to be very effective," says Elise Rollinson, corporate relations manager, Volunteer San Diego (San Diego, CA), an affiliate of the Hands On Network. "Some basic preparation can turn a few hours of labor or support into significant contributions to a community or charitable agency."

The first step is determining the training required.

"The training necessary will depend greatly on the type of volunteer project or activity the employee is participating in," Rollinson says. "If a corporate volunteer is offering a skill-based or pro-bono volunteer service such as technical, marketing, legal or accounting support, then there could be a significant time commitment and skill set required to get up to speed on the agencies' information and needs. With a 'done in a day' beautification or engagement type volunteer project, it makes the most sense to train some project leaders in advance of the project. With a few key leaders familiar with the project goals, supplies and timeline, the project will be much more organized and effective."

Although the type of training varies depending on the project, Rollinson says there are topics to always address:

- **Project details.** Inform corporate volunteers in advance about who they are supporting, the project's details, how to dress, what to bring and confidentiality.
- **Organizational information.** Inform corporate volunteers about your nonprofit's work by inviting your executive director to talk about your organization's needs, mission and future volunteer opportunities.
- **Corporate giving.** Rollinson recommends inviting the CEO or corporate manager to address the volunteers. "By explaining the corporate giving guidelines or employee volunteer program, from the corporate perspective, it will help them understand the purpose of the volunteer project."
- **Client needs.** Be sure the volunteers have some understanding of the population they are supporting. Discuss the needs and challenges of your clients.
- **The volunteer's role.** Provide written instructions so each volunteer has a clear understanding of their responsibilities. Include information such as the project's goals, the tools required and helpful skills.

As corporate volunteers learn about your organization, the clients you service and the project itself, Rollinson says it is important to be respectful of the volunteer's time, comfort level and skill set. Help your volunteer find a job that suits them. The feeling of accomplishment and support is what will make them volunteer again and again.

Source: Elise Rollinson, Corporate Relations Manager, Volunteer San Diego, San Diego, CA. Phone (858) 636-4128. E-mail: erollinson@volunteersandiego.org

Train Episodic Volunteers for Effective Results

Episodic volunteers can be vital to organizations requiring short-term assistance for event planning or the administration of short-term volunteering tasks. With multiple demands for their time, many volunteers opt to become an episodic volunteer in order to fulfill personal goals in a less demanding timeframe.

Courtney Dodd, extension program specialist, Texas AgriLife Extension (College Station, TX), offers the following guidelines to garner the most effective episodic volunteer training and management approach:

Determine how their talents will be utilized:

- Discuss with staff and long-term volunteers the best use of your episodic volunteers time.
- Develop meaningful ways in which episodic volunteers can contribute. These volunteers hunger for hands-on activities.

Create a support structure that offers success:

- Develop brief training or orientation sessions for this unique group of volunteers. Typically, a 15-minute training or orientation session will suffice for an episodic volunteer.
- Train specifically for the event or task assigned. Offer an abbreviated review of the organization's expectations.
- Give clear direction and assign them a supervisor. Before the volunteer's arrival, create pocket-sized cards that contain a brief description of their duty and their supervisor's name. Distribute at orientation. They will serve as a quick refernce guide for the volunteer.
- Ask long-term volunteers to act as team captains to manage and train episodic volunteers.

Offer flexibility:

- Offer volunteer opportunities that are convenient for them.

Present feedback:

- Solicit and compile feedback from event attendees or recipients, captains and episodic volunteers to share with the episodic volunteers to bolster their desire to return for other volunteer efforts within your organization.
- Feedback allows them to see the impact of their work.

Source: Courtney Dodd, Extension Program Specialist, Texas AgriLife Extension Service, College Station, TX. Phone (979) 845-6533. E-mail: CFDodd@ag.tamu.edu

Volunteer Training Primer: Principles, Procedures and Ideas for Training and Educating Volunteers.
Edited by Scott C. Stevenson.
© 2009 Stevenson, Inc. Published 2009 by Stevenson, Inc.

ADDITIONAL TRAINING CONSIDERATIONS

This final chapter covers some critical training topics not addressed in previous chapters. For example, what can you do to keep training costs in line? How can you prepare your volunteers for a disaster? How can you train existing volunteers to mentor new recruits? These and other topics will be addressed here.

Ways to Keep Training Costs in Line

Here are tips from two national volunteer organizations on how to keep volunteer training costs down.

1. Place a "Property of …" sticker on the back of training manuals to remind volunteers to return them.

2. Give one chapter of the manual at a time so those who don't finish the training won't have the entire manual.

3. For lengthy manual chapters, give volunteers a summary and keep the entire chapter available in your office for a reference.

4. Contact local colleges, city and government offices and newspapers for in-kind services and support for printing materials.

5. Laminate items you plan to reuse.

   — *National CASA (Court Appointed Special Advocates for Children), www.nationalcasa.org*

6. Engage your experienced volunteers as trainers and save on staffing costs.

7. Approach local bagel shops, coffee houses and sandwich makers for donations or discounts on refreshments for trainees.

8. Ask your local copy shop to donate or discount the cost of printing training manuals. Provide your originals in advance so they can print your job during slow periods.

9. Publish training resources and reference guides on your website and save on printing costs.

10. For volunteers who are geographically dispersed, use online meeting tools to conduct web-based training. Ask a corporate sponsor to host your online training using their technology and save on license fees or use a free service such as Empower.

11. For specialized training (e.g., health-related skills), it may be cheaper to pay someone to train your volunteers. Check with other nonprofits offering similar training to see if they would include your volunteers in their classes for a small fee.

   — *The Points of Light Foundation and Volunteer Center National Network, www.PointsofLight.org*

Restructured Training Improves Volunteer Retention

Volunteers are introduced to numerous facets of your program through the training process. Danilo Minnick, director of volunteer services and student recruitment, Literacy Partners (New York, NY), notes that a restructured training program can help improve volunteer retention.

In 2002, only 19 percent of his volunteer tutor trainees met the required one-year commitment. Once the Literacy Partners application process was streamlined and the training process improved, 40 percent remained active for one to two years and 13 percent volunteered two or more years.

The number of volunteer "red flags" has also decreased, retention of trainees is between 90 and 95 percent, tutored students demonstrate greater educational gains, and the training program received national accreditation by ProLiteracy America (making it the only adult literacy program in New York City to receive this distinction).

Training sessions were previously held on an unscheduled basis, which made it more difficult to fill the meetings with qualified volunteers; a poorly written training manual didn't prepare volunteers for the tasks at hand. The schedule, resources and training structure have been changed. Four-week quarterly sessions were established. The committee also revised and divided the training manual into sections: teaching strategies, reading, writing, math and resources. New teaching practices give trainees more hands-on experience, including working in groups, on-site observations and making a presentation at the end of the training session. Volunteers provided immediate positive feedback once these changes were in place.

Volunteers also offer suggestions for further improvements in the training process. Their suggestions, which help keep the training relevant and timely, are also a catalyst for change.

Sources: Danilo Minnick, Director of Volunteer Services & Student Recruitment, Alexa Titus, Director of Education, Literacy Partners, New York, NY. Phone (212) 715-9200.
E-mail: danilom@literacypartners.org

ADDITIONAL TRAINING CONSIDERATIONS

Maintain a Complete Training Record

Training records are an important part of any volunteer program. These records may prove essential, either because of certain government or insurance regulations or to lessen potential liability risk.

Here are tips for starting or improving training records for your volunteers.

Maintain confidentiality. Be sure only those with a need to know have access to any information concerning your volunteers, including their training.

List the tasks for each position. For example, one task in the gift shop might be to operate the cash register. A task for tour guides could be having knowledge about a certain display.

Have both trainer and trainee sign and date each task when training is complete. This should eliminate any possibility of a volunteer saying he/she wasn't trained on a certain task.

Review volunteer training records periodically. Set up a schedule of reviews according to the organization's size and complexity. Go over the records with volunteers to see if they need to repeat or add to part of their training.

Paid Training Leads to Highly Committed Volunteers

At Lindsay Wildlife Museum (Walnut Creek, CA), volunteers are asked to pay training fees and to become museum members, says Patti Harris, education director. The fees, she says, help offset costs while ensuring volunteers are serious about their commitment.

The museum's 60 volunteer docents provide programs for elementary school children at the museum and in classroom. The volunteers offer concept-based, age-appropriate educational opportunities based on the California Science standards.

The complex nature of working with live animals, as well as local laws, requires docents be 18 and older, says Harris. Additionally, the goal of the museum is to select committed, long-term volunteers because of the complexity of the training.

"Almost all of our volunteer opportunities are long-term commitments," Harris says. "We provide more than 20 hours of initial training for docents in the first year. In addition, our docents are expected to attend monthly continuing education meetings."

The introductory docent class is $8 for members and $10 for non-members. Extended training is $65 for members and $100 for non-members, which includes membership. Scholarships are available to those who cannot afford the training fees.

Source: Patti Harris, Education Director, Walnut Creek, CA. Phone (925) 935-1978. E-mail: pharris@wildlife-museum.org

Don't Forget to Cover Fire Drill Basics

When was the last time you conducted a fire drill? If it's been a while, you may want to review these fire drill basics:

1. Conduct drills regularly. Because building occupants may change from year to year, you should conduct at least one fire drill a year.

2. Vary the hazards encountered in your drill. For example:

   • Place a drawing of flames or a cardboard cutout to show a fire in a particular area. Occupants must evacuate based on the location of the fire.

   • Post a sign inside one of the exit stairwells stating that it is blocked by fire, smoke or debris and that a different exit must be used.

3. Hold an evaluation session following each drill with building occupants, if possible, and your crisis management team to discuss what went wrong and what went right during the drill.

Prepare Volunteers For a Disaster

Are your volunteers prepared to handle a disaster if one should strike tomorrow? Whether it would be a tornado, flood or earthquake, it is important volunteers receive appropriate training in disaster preparedness.

Schedule a two- or three-day training where volunteers can learn the basic dos and don'ts when put in the middle of a natural disaster.

Ask your local emergency responders (e.g., EMTs, firefighters, and police) to take part in your training session, sharing expertise and answering volunteer questions.

If your organization has a large number of volunteers offer several training sessions from which they can choose to attend, but make them a requirement.

By showing your volunteers today how to prepare for the unexpected, you will create a disaster-ready and able volunteer who is ready to assist when asked to meet the call to action.

ADDITIONAL TRAINING CONSIDERATIONS

Medical Center Masters Online Volunteer Orientation

To simplify the orientation process for you and your volunteers, offer it online.

Rather than requiring volunteers to sit through a face-to-face orientation session, an online orientation allows them to work at their own pace in a comfortable setting.

Plus, it makes tracking information much easier for your organization.

Volunteer coordinators at the University of Arkansas for Medical Sciences Medical Center (UAMS) of Little Rock, AR, began an online volunteer orientation a year ago.

Andrea Stokes, former volunteer coordinator and creator of its online orientation, says that when a volunteer's application is received electronically, he/she is asked to complete the online orientation. To do so, volunteers:

- Read through an online version of the volunteer manual. It covers topics ranging from safety codes to policies and procedures to the history of UAMS.

- Complete four tests and/or forms relating directly to material studied: HIPAA, confidentiality, safety and a volunteer contract.

- Receive an e-mail thanking them for completing the orientation and directing them to contact the volunteer department to schedule an interview.

"Essentially and ideally, all interested volunteers who have scheduled an interview have already completed their online orientation session and have an idea of the way UAMS operates, its history and its mission," Stokes explains.

To ensure a participant actually completes the orientation, she says:

- A database tracks each component of the orientation session.

- Applicants take tests to fully ensure they have read and understand the material.

- All volunteer applicants must interview with a staff member. During this time, the staff member evaluates the applicant's skill sets.

Source: Andrea Stokes, Clinical Research Promoter, Arkansas Children's Hospital, Little Rock, AR. Phone (501) 364-3309. E-mail: stokesandreac@uams.edu. Website: www.archildrens.org

---

Create a Successful Volunteer Orientation — Online

Andrea Stokes, former volunteer coordinator, University of Arkansas for Medical Sciences Medical Center (Little Rock, AR), offers the following advice for organizations interested in starting an online orientation process:

1. **Ignore the belief that online orientation only appeals to people in a specific age bracket.** "People from every generation are willing to try this out as long as you are patient with your instructions and make your module easy to find and easy to understand," she explains.

2. **Be meticulous when editing your website and orientation module.** Stokes says it is important to create a friendly and welcoming look. Additionally, avoid spelling and grammatical errors.

3. **Be prepared to edit and update.** "There is nothing worse than a website that hasn't been edited in more than a year," Stokes says. "If your uniforms have changed, change your pictures. If your confidentiality statement has been revised, don't forget to revise it in your orientation materials. You don't want to mislead volunteers."

4. **Use lots of guinea pigs.** Stokes recommends going through the materials monthly to make sure everything is working properly and is user-friendly.

5. **Invest in a good database.** "Volunteer tracking is essential to maintaining any volunteer program, especially when you are using an online system that may attract individuals who never become volunteers," Stokes says. "Keep all records and, if you can, track all correspondence you make with potential applicants via e-mail, your website, telephone, etc. It's helpful to have those records when you hear from them again."

ADDITIONAL TRAINING CONSIDERATIONS

Successful Phone Training Techniques

Incorporate the customer service expectations of your organization when training volunteers to answer phones.

Mary Pengra, director, volunteer services, Sacred Heart Hospital (Eau Claire, WI), says customer service training is an essential part of training information desk volunteers. Information desk volunteers greet the public in person and on the phone. They give patient information and direct the public to different hospital areas.

Pengra says the best customer service advice they give their volunteers is to always wear a smile, especially while on the phone, because that attitude carries through.

The complete phone training includes:

1. The general volunteer orientation.

2. An orientation to discuss hospital information and customer service.

3. A required staff training on the hospital's basic customer service skill set.

4. Training with a staff person for a minimum of two shifts where volunteers each learn phone and computer system mechanics, how to handle calls and face-to-face public interaction.

5. Ongoing training with an experienced volunteer.

6. On-the-job coaching and constructive, positive feedback.

Source: Mary Pengra, Director, Volunteer Services, Sacred Heart Hospital, Eau Claire, WI. Phone (715) 839-4074. E-mail: mpengra@shec.hshs.org

Get Existing Members To Mentor New Recruits

The "buddy principle" — pairing up existing members with new ones — often serves as a good way to help new members learn more about your organization and get involved at the same time. This mentor system also has the added benefit of keeping your existing members involved in a meaningful way.

To begin a member mentor program or build upon an existing one, consider these ideas:

1. Host a reception for new and existing members. After everyone has had an opportunity to socialize, publicly invite those in attendance to pair up with someone (veteran members with new recruits). This gives members the opportunity to partner with someone of their own choosing.

2. Provide buddy pairs with a checklist of "assignments" that should be completed by a particular date — an informal tour of the facility, at least one meal together, a review of opportunities for member involvement, etc. This shared checklist will help keep the new member and mentor more accountable to one another.

3. Allow the mentor the opportunity of presenting the new member with a surprise benefit of some sort: an invitation to a special exhibit or a special members only reception.

4. To help members get to know members, consider a four-week or four-month program in which new members and their mentors are switched to another partner every week or month for four different times.

Three Ways to Educate, Inspire Mentors

Are you in search of creative training methods for volunteer mentors? Betsy McCauley, district volunteer specialist, Leon County Schools (Tallahassee, FL), identifies three techniques she uses to educate volunteer mentors:

1. **Role play** — McCauley chooses two mentors during the training and role plays some "real life mentor situations" that always arise before they ever meet with a student. "I pretend to be the mentor and talk with them like they are students," she says. "It allows the trainer to bring up delicate topics in a safe environment and allows mentors to see there are simple solutions to overcome these issues."

2. **Walk 'n Talk** — This exercise demonstrates how important even the smallest amount of time (e.g., walk from a classroom to the media center) is with a child. "Week to week mentors have to rebond with students," says McCauley. "During the walk is the mentor's time to talk with the child about their interests (e.g., basketball, a new t-shirt, movies, etc.) and reconnect with them."

3. **Fisherman** — "It is the mentor's job to be the fisherman and keep casting until they find out the student's interests and what lights up the child," she says. "Once the mentors uncover a child's interest (e.g., dinosaurs, astronomy, nature, etc.), they can then get them excited about education."

Source: Betsy McCauley, District Volunteer Specialist, Leon County Schools, Tallahassee, FL. Phone (850) 487-4321. E-mail: mccauleyb@mail.leon.k12.fl.us

Lightning Source UK Ltd.
Milton Keynes UK
UKOW011859280613

212924UK00006B/166/P